C

Timothy Hall is a freelance journalist and the author of more than fifty books. He is a former correspondent for the *London Observer* and the *BBC* and has also written extensively for the *Bulletin* and for *Reader's Digest*. Much of his work involves investigative journalism and his exposure of the mining industry's deliberate concealment of the dangers of asbestos was the first to alert the community to this problem.

THE FALL
OF
SINGAPORE

Timothy Hall

MANDARIN
AUSTRALIA

For my godfather, Alan Simpson

Published 1990 by
Mandarin Australia
an imprint of the Octopus Publishing Group
a division of Reed International Books Australia Pty Ltd
22 Salmon Street, Port Melbourne, Victoria 3207

Reprinted 1992

First published 1983 by
Methuen Australia Pty Ltd

Printed and bound in Australia by
Griffin Paperbacks

National Library of Australia
  cataloguing-in-publication data:

Hall, Timothy, 1938– .
   The fall of Singapore.

   Bibliography.
   Includes index.
   ISBN 1 86330 043 0.

   1. World War, 1939–1945 – Campaigns – Asia, Southeastern.
   2. Singapore – History – Siege, 1942. I. Title.
940.5425

Contents

Acknowledgements

I am grateful to many who served in the Malayan Campaign, and their families, who gave me their time and who so kindly made available to me diaries and letters. In Singapore I was given every assistance by the Singapore Government and I owe a special debt to Singapore Airlines who carried me in both directions with much friendliness and help.

Mrs Cynthia Koek enthralled me with her memories of the days before and after the capitulation.

The Australian War Memorial was, as always, invaluable. If any errors have crept in, they are my responsibility and mine alone.

Introduction

Extending down from Burma and Thailand until it almost touches the great island of Sumatra is the long narrow appendix of land which is the Malay Peninsula. Since ancient times it has formed a physical and cultural link between the mainland and islands of the East Indies.

Along the length of its spine runs a mountain range, rising at its peak to 2287 m, and covered for the most part with dense jungle. On either side of these mountains, the land levels off into the low-lying coastal plains. Monsoon rains, which give Malaya an annual rainfall of 2500 mm, most of it falling in torrential downpours, have resulted in dense evergreen rainforests which even today cover 60 per cent of the country.

Flying over Malaya, it is hard to see why this small country — hardly as large as England and Wales — should have been prized by anyone, but beneath the green canopy lay boundless wealth. As the world geared up for war in 1939 and 1940, Malaya was the world's largest producer of two of the most vital primary products in any war, tin and rubber. And in the production of palm oil, a valuable oil used for making soap, candles and lubricating grease, Malaya was second only to Nigeria.

At the very toe of the peninsula, dominating one of the most important trade routes in the world, lay the Crown Colony island of Singapore, the visible symbol of the power and invincibility of the British Empire in the Far East.

For the Japanese, scheming to extend their hegemony throughout the Far East, the subjugation of Malaya and Singapore was a key move in their elaborate game. The avowed Japanese aim was to establish what they termed euphemistically 'The Greater East-Asia Co-Prosperity Sphere', an economic system independent of sterling, the American dollar and the rest of the world, with Japan herself, of course, as its nucleus. At all times this conception of becoming a master race was common to the German and the Japanese leaders and coloured their entire strategy.

Singapore was singled out to be the capital of the Co-Prosperity Sphere's southern region and was to be the chief military supply base in the area. In the process, its subjugation would see the removal once and for all of the most visible and obnoxious bastion of British domination in the area.

For Australia the island had a special significance because its continuing role as an allied base was crucial to the very existence of Australia itself. If the Japanese held Singapore, they would also control the sea lanes; and if they controlled the sea lanes, they could starve Australia into submission without a single Japanese life being risked in an armed invasion.

Ever since 1819 when Thomas Stamford Raffles had acquired the steaming jungle island for Great Britain, it was assumed that any threat to Singapore would come from the sea. The mountainous jungle of Malaya to the north and beyond that again in Thailand and Burma, seemed to Britain's strategists to be a natural defence that no man-made fortifications could improve upon.

Britain therefore concentrated on constructing a series of elaborate fixed defences which were all aimed at protecting Singapore against an amphibious attack. These defences, including five huge 15-inch naval rifles, six 9.2-inch guns and eighteen 6-inch guns, made the expression 'Fortress' seem entirely appropriate, and the phrase 'Fortress of Singapore' slipped effortlessly into the vocabulary.

After World War I, when Japan was perceived as a major threat to Britain's possessions in the Far East, it was decided to strengthen its position by the construction of a huge naval base. It would occupy a large part of the northern coast of Singapore Island and cost $60 million. This base, with its huge dockyard, would be the key to Britain's naval supremacy in the Far East. Sprawling over some 60 sq km, it was large enough to take the entire British fleet at the same time and it included two enormous 50 000 tonne dry docks.

Once people began referring to it as the Fortress, it was only a short step to accepting that it was also as impregnable as a fortress; and this uncritical acceptance that Singapore could withstand any attack, coupled with the belief that such an attack would only come from the sea, persisted for so long that by 1940, when a real threat arose for the first time in more than a century, it was accepted almost as divine writ. Certainly no one questioned it at the levels that mattered on the island itself, in London or in Canberra.

From Britain's point of view, there were many advantages in her enemies, as well as the local population, believing that Singapore was impregnable. The British government (which thought it was true anyway) remained convinced that it would help deter the Japanese from attempting an attack. Unlike the British and the islanders, however, the Japanese knew precisely what the state of the defences of the island was. They had an excellent intelligence service, and throughout Malaya and Singapore there were loyal Japanese working in a variety of jobs.

They owned iron mines and rubber estates, fortuitously located near strategically important places. They operated freighters from the east coast of Malaya and Singapore up to Japan and so could keep a close watch on defence activities as well as acquiring an intimate knowledge of the coast line. Japanese sales representatives moved around freely and many of the professional photographers in Singapore were Japanese, an ideal set up for espionage. All passed information back to Tokyo.

The Planning Chief at Imperial Army Headquarters in Tokyo, in particular, was convinced that attack from the sea, which meant from the east, south or west, was impossible. 'Attack is possible only from the Johore Strait, north of Singapore', he wrote, and from that moment there was never any question in the Japanese minds that their invasion would be launched from that direction.

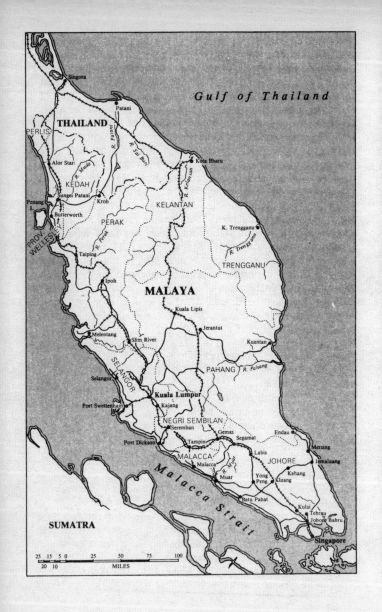

The Impregnable Fortress

It had taken the Japanese planners three days, in September 1940, to satisfy themselves that Singapore could only be safely attacked from the mainland. Posing as business executives on vacation, the Japanese Planning Chief and an aide had driven all over the island and had hired a boat from which they could see the lie of the land from the water.

Unfortunately the Allied defence planners, perhaps blinded by the obvious, were not so logical in their reasoning and what took the Japanese three days to work out, was still eluding them when the Japanese convoys set sail for Malaya more than a year later.

No one appeared even remotely concerned at the vulnerability of Singapore and as early as the end of September 1939, the Chiefs of Staff in London had increased their estimate of the time that the garrison in Singapore would have to hold out for before relief came, to 180 days. At that time, too, the air force was so weak that it consisted of only five poorly equipped squadrons to which a sixth was added shortly afterwards.

When the commanders of the military and air garrisons in Singapore, who were beginning to feel uncomfortably vulnerable, asked London for reinforcements, they were told that no one could be spared. Instead the General Officer Commanding Malaya at the time, Lieutenant General Sir Lionel Bond, was told that if he wanted to increase his strength, he should improve the efficiency of the Volunteers. A local home-guard-type force, a third of whose establishment was European numbering less than 2400, the majority of the Volunteers were Chinese and Malays. But the British government also told the Malay government that its first priority was not defence but the rubber and tin industries which were producing badly needed American dollars. No volunteers could therefore be taken from among experienced managers and technicians on either the plantations or the tin mines.

The collapse of France in June 1940 altered the whole picture. The strength of Singapore and therefore the security of Australia relied primarily on a pre-war undertaking by Britain that a British squadron of capital ships would proceed to Singapore immediately there were any hostilities in the Far East or the Pacific that threatened either Australia, New Zealand or Singapore itself.

The assumption was that the British fleet would sail quickly for the Far East leaving the French fleet to take care of the powerful Italian fleet in the Mediterranean. But now, if Britain moved its Mediterranean fleet, there would be nothing left to contain the Italian navy which would be free to operate in the Atlantic with impunity or to reinforce the German fleet in home waters, using bases in north-west France which it now controlled. Britain didn't have a large enough fleet to do both jobs.

For a year before the Japanese entered the war, Allied service leaders squabbled at top level about whether the garrison of Singapore should be concentrated on the island or deployed partly on the Malayan mainland. The Air Force argued that in the absence of a fleet, Malaya would have to rely mainly on air power and that therefore the army must defend airfields far and wide through Malaya. It had already been decided by the Chiefs of Staff that reliance would have to be placed chiefly on air power and that the whole of Malaya and Singapore had to be defended.

By mid-October 1940 the three service chiefs in Malaya, in a joint appreciation to the Chiefs of Staff, confirmed that the aeroplane would be the principal weapon for defending Malaya, and that its task would be to repulse any invading force while it was still at sea, break up any attempts at landings and attack any troops who managed to get ashore. In this way, the Allies would not be forced to meet the Japanese in a major ground confrontation.

The estimate of the minimum number of aircraft needed to defend Singapore and Burma was 534 modern aircraft, yet throughout both countries, there were exactly 88 and only 48 of these were classed as modern. Back in Australia there were another 82, but only 42 of these were modern; and New Zealand and other countries in the Indian Ocean had 4, all obsolete.

Inter-service bickering and rivalry continued to plague all three services over the Far East question and was becoming increasingly counter-productive. For nearly fifteen years the service chiefs in London had been arguing about the best way of defending the new naval base with the Air Force proposing that aircraft should be used, which they claimed could attack an enemy before it came within range of the big guns; and the Navy and Army wanting heavy fixed armaments to repel an attack from the sea where they were convinced lay the only threat to the island.

The Army and Navy had won, but the co-operation between all three services after that deteriorated visibly and distressingly for those who watched it. The Army insisted that no enemy could ever advance down the Malay Peninsula; the Air Force agreed that the Japanese might not come down overland, but believed they could certainly come down by air.

The Air Force therefore began constructing airfields up-country as early as 1936 in an assortment of places, many of them almost inaccessible to anyone but a team of explorers. But because it expected no co-operation from it, it made no attempt to consult with the Army which would have the responsibility of defending them and which in fact promptly insisted that most of them had been built in the wrong place anyway.

In October 1940, mainly to try and resolve this unhappy situation, the British government appointed a man as Commander-in-Chief, Far East, who had a background as soldier, airman and civil administrator which it was felt might allow him to so dominate the other personalities that the rift would be healed. Nothing could have been further from the truth.

Air Chief Marshal Sir Robert Brooke-Popham was sixty-two when he was brought back on to the active list from Kenya where he was Governor. For the first fourteen years in his career he had been an infantry officer and had then transferred to the Flying Corps in World War I. He had risen to the rank of Air Chief Marshal and had left the service to take up the appointment in Kenya.

Brooke-Popham arrived in Singapore on 14 November 1940, a tall and distinguished looking man who had no illusions about the difficulty of the job that faced him. His responsibility was unusual in the British services in that he was commanding both the Air Force and the Army throughout the Far East.

At sixty-two however he was relatively old for an active command and the Australian Resident Minister in Singapore, V. G. Bowden, in a letter to the Secretary of the Department of External Affairs in Australia, described him as a man who showed 'an extraordinary diffidence of manner for a man in his position', and who was 'definitely too old for such a position in wartime'.

Brooke-Popham's main obstacle to restoring any kind of harmony was that he had no control over the Navy in spite of the fact that the approaches to his areas of responsibility were largely by sea. So Singapore found itself in the ridiculous situation of having two Commanders-in-Chief, each responsible to a different authority in London.

The Combined Intelligence Bureau on which each of the three services relied for information of Japanese intentions and troop movements, remained under the control of the Navy and not of Brooke-Popham, and the Navy showed itself remarkably reluctant to share all its information.

The Army and Air Force had their own intelligence services of sorts, but they did not have the resources of the Combined Intelligence Bureau for collecting and interpreting information that they obtained.

Civil administration, although obviously essential for the defence of Malaya and Singapore, was again specifically kept outside Brooke-Popham's area of responsibility, in spite of the fact that he had shown himself to be an able administrator in Africa; and even more seriously, he was told not to take on administrative or financial responsibilities or even the normal day-to-day functions of an Army or Air Force Commander. He was thus effectively isolated from the real business of being a commander. Instead he was to concentrate exclusively on matters of major military strategy and policy, though again not on political matters which still had to be referred back to London.

Brooke-Popham lasted in the job until only 27 December 1941 when he was replaced by an army officer with much more up-to-date experience, Lieutenant-General Sir Henry Pownall. Brooke-Popham's unhappy tenure cannot have been made easier by the leaking of the information that he was to be replaced almost a month before it happened.

In early 1941, the Allies had a major break-through when the Americans cracked the Japanese code that was being used for secret communications between Japan and the United States. In this way, they learned as early as 1941 what had until then been conjecture; that Japan was contemplating acquiring military bases in Indo-China and Thailand, and ultimately attacking Singapore.

In spite of this, there were still significant differences of opinion between Churchill and his military advisers on the relative importance to the Empire of the Middle East and Malaya in Britain's overall strategy. Churchill still believed that the likelihood of Japan entering the war was remote; but that if she did, America would come in on Britain's side, bringing with her the mighty navy that she had built up, so that there was no need for Britain to do any more about the defence of Malaya and Singapore beyond what he accurately called 'the modest arrangements already in progress'.

His Chief of General Staff and operational planners disagreed with him. In one report they conceded that the threat in the Far East was still only potential and that others nearer home were more grimly real. But they saw this as a deception. 'Should it develop,' the Chief of Staff wrote, 'this threat may bring even greater dangers than those we now face. It is vital to take, as soon as possible, the necessary measures to secure the defence of Singapore.'

If they had known what was being discussed in Berlin at about this time, they would have been doubly concerned and looked even more suspiciously on the amiable, smiling Japanese negotiators who seemed intent only on assuring Britain that she had nothing to fear.

Yosuke Matsuoka, the Japanese Foreign Minister, had travelled there for a meeting with his German counterpart, Joachim von Ribbentrop, whom he assured that Japan was doing everything possible to reassure the British about Singapore and lull them into a false sense of security. It might be possible that his attitude towards the English could even appear to be friendly in words and acts, he told von Ribbentrop, who was probably the most ardent anglophobe in the German government; but Germany should not be deceived by that.

He said that he was assuming this attitude not only to reassure the British, but also to fool the pro-British and pro-American elements until one day he would suddenly open the attack on Singapore.

Von Ribbentrop was pleased to hear this. The previous

September he had signed a Tripartite Pact with Japan and Italy, providing for mutual assistance against the United States. And Hitler had decreed that it must be the aim of the collaboration between the three countries to induce the Japanese as soon as possible to take active measures in the Far East.

The German High Command was ordered to co-operate to the fullest extent with the Japanese and among the guiding principles that Hitler laid down and expected to be observed, was that the seizure of Singapore as the key British position in the Far East, would represent a decisive victory for all three powers.

In spite of the Pact there had lingered considerable suspicion by both Germany and Japan as to the intentions of the other, and von Ribbentrop found it very reassuring to hear from the Japanese minister that all his posturing was nothing more than that, and that Japan was just biding its time to pounce.

The Australian government's original plan had been to send a brigade group to Malaya where it would be directly under Malaya Command, but this had been changed. With the brigade would now go part of Divisional Headquarters as well on the grounds that normal brigade staff would be unable to handle an Australian force overseas.

Had this not been decided, the brigade would have been denied its remarkable brigadier; the Allies would have been deprived of one of their most aggressive and controversial commanders in the campaign; and the Japanese would have been spared the Australian they most feared in the Malayan campaign. Major General Gordon Bennett left an ineradicable mark on Australia's military history and the passage of time has still not fully resolved the question of whether he was more wronged or wrong-doer.

A small advance party of the brigade left on 31 January 1941 and on 2 February the rest of the unit followed. They embarked on the 81 000-tonne *Queen Mary*, now drab in her camouflage paint as a troop carrier and anonymously renamed simply *H.T.Q.X.*, and took their place in a convoy that included the liners *Aquitania* and *Nieuw Amsterdam*. Their escort was the Australian cruiser *Hobart*.

In all 12 000 members of the AIF were in the convoy, about 5500 on the *Queen Mary* bound for Singapore and the rest destined for the Middle East. Commanding the 22nd Brigade was Brigadier H. B. Taylor, a Government Analyst, and the brigade included the 2/18th, 2/19th and 2/20th Battalions with an array of supporting units, from an anti-tank regiment, to a mobile bacteriological laboratory, a dental unit and a provost company.

The troops destined for Malaya were known as Elbow Force and the Army went to considerable lengths to keep their destination secret. They appear to have succeeded in spite of truck loads of crates marked Elbow Force, Singapore, which arrived at the wharf for loading on to the ship; the men had been at sea for nine days before they were told their final destination. There were some moving scenes as the convoy divided, the two smaller liners to go onto the Middle East. Men lined the rails, shouting and cheering as the ships whooped mournfully and slipped away in opposite directions.

The *Queen Mary* arrived in Singapore on 18 February and the brigade disembarked, each man trying to take in the sights and smells and sounds of this utterly new world. Few had ever travelled outside Australia before.

Whatever most of them had expected, it had certainly not included the Europeans they saw. They were expecting to be in action within a fortnight and there were rumours that they might be at the battle-front much sooner than that, yet even in the short time they were in Singapore, they saw people enjoying a social life that would have been lavish in peace time. In the evening they saw officers resplendent in mess kit, and fashionable women laughing and chatting in long evening dresses yet this was supposed to be a war posting.

Remembering this first encounter, one brigade officer wrote later, 'It was not only incongruous, it was wrong. Either we were crazy or they were crazy. Either there was danger or there was no danger. If the latter, why had we been sent there? And why were more troops on the way from India?'

They were hard questions for anyone suddenly dropped on to the Singapore scene to answer.

The happy accident of time, which positioned Singapore at the cross-roads of two of the world's great trade routes, assured it a prosperity that had few equals. And for those Europeans who lived there, it offered a life-style that had already been long forgotten by most Britons slogging out the post-Depression years at home.

Wars, tribulation and economic disasters might trouble the lives of others, but in Singapore they hardly ruffled the surface. The whole of World War I might almost not have happened for all the difference that it had made to those on Singapore. Life remained, as it did for the first two years of the Second World War, very, very agreeable.

Singapore's fortunes had changed suddenly when the Suez Canal opened in 1869. Few people had cause to be so grateful to de Lesseps, for the canal brought to the little island the age of the steamship and with it undreamed of prosperity. Even more than Malaya had been for centuries before, it became the cross-roads of South-East Asia and as a free port, open to ships of all nations, one of the greatest ports in the world.

It quickly became the main outlet for Malaya's tin and rubber exports, and as the country was producing half of all the world's tin and rubber output, it was an enormously profitable exercise. Right up until 1939, Singapore was essentially a fortress of British colonial trade.

The Europeans, who lived a Somerset Maugham type of existence, were there for the most part as traders, administrators or missionaries. It was also the distribution and leave centre for many of the Europeans up-country, particularly the lonely planters on the mainland.

The British, whatever their intelligence or background, lived a life of pampered luxury. By day the civil servants, worked in their ostentatious and imposing offices, clustered together in the heart of white Singapore. And at night, surrounded comfortingly by their own people, they closed out the rest of the world and enjoyed themselves, untroubled for the most part by the slightest pangs of conscience about the lot of the Asians on the other side of the wall.

Raffles, that most nostalgically named hotel in the world, was the centre of Singapore's white social life and Maugham wasn't exaggerating when he said of it, 'It stands for all the fables of the exotic east.'

If the number of those who could dine out on having met C. M. Phillips, the celebrated headmaster who had disturbed a tiger under the billiard table at Raffles, was dwindling, at least under the 90-foot travellers palms, they could sip lazily at their gin slings and *stengahs*.

Raffles was traditionally the domain of the British in the colony — and in those intolerant days, British meant white and never mind what it said on the front of the passport — and many of the other nationalities had their own equivalent. The Germans, for example, built their own Teutonia Club, an extraordinary building off Orchard Road, modelled on a Rhine castle. Before it was turned into another famous Singapore landmark, the Goodwood Park Hotel, it was the scene of nearly as many balls and banquets as Raffles.

There were also a number of clubs, exclusively European of course, which were frequented as much for their social life as for their main purpose. Typical was the Cricket Club, almost rustic in appearance, at one end of the *padang*, the huge open sports area at the end of town.

Down near the water was the other face of the city, the great sprawling, bustling and colourful Asian metropolis, as far removed as one could imagine from the green suburbs to the north of the city where the spacious bungalows of the richer Europeans shielded them from the real world outside.

In Chinatown, little had changed since the turn of the century. Outside the tiny shops, with their silks and brasses, exotic foods and cage birds, the hawkers plied their wares from dawn till long after dusk. The Chinese crowded into the houses that from the sunlit streets looked dark and mysterious, every window festooned with washing, strung out on poles to dry like grubby flags left out for too long after a parade. Behind the windows the shadowy figures of old men and women looked down on the activity.

Yet Chinatown, for all its colour and charm, was a notorious slum. In one street, Upper Nankin Street, only 200 m long, 1800 people lived in the two- and three- storeyed shop-houses. They lived in cubicles, each adult on average with 9 square metres of space, often with four to a cubicle. Many had no window. For all this population there were 105 lavatories, all of the open bucket type and many next to the cooking space. It was as well that not too many of the visitors to Chinatown looked past the facade.

The Chinese secret societies proliferated in spite of various ordinances and an Act of Supression, but they were a far more potent source of cohesion among the Chinese community than the white government when the emergency began.

The Chinese streets were crowded with carts and gharries, trishaws and trucks, but walk a few paces and suddenly you found yourself in a part of the city where life was much more leisurely, this time the domain of the Indians, their women in brilliant saris never far away.

And around almost every corner there was the sea or the curling Singapore River, the water almost hidden under the mass of sampans on which whole families were born and lived and died. Among the sampans again were the barges which carried cargo between the docks and freighters in the harbour. And along the deep water channel known as Keppel Harbour, were miles of berths, warehouses and go-downs.

Two imposing white edifices, one to God, the other to his right-hand man, the Governor, dominated in their own way a corner of the city. And both survived the war more or less intact.

At Government House, the palatial building stood in its own park-like grounds, with trees dotting the great expanse of lawn and giving it shade as it sloped down to the gates. And the extraordinary cathedral of St Andrews, gleaming white like an immense concoction in ice and sugar — extraordinary because of its construction, for inside it was cool and peaceful.

St Andrews was built by convicts who used lime mixed not with sand, but with egg white and sugar beaten to a paste. This in turn was mixed with water in which coconut husks had been soaked and after the resulting plaster had been applied and dried, it was rubbed with rock crystal until it shone and sparkled like marble.

There was a good road network in Singapore — as there was throughout Malaya where the British constructed roads with the zeal of the colonising Romans in Britain 1900 years before. Most parts of the island were accessible and the main highway, the Bukit Timah Road, ran north-west out of the city and then turned north to join up with the causeway where it became the main trunk road through Malaya to Thailand and Burma.

The Bukit Timah Road was not as straight in 1941 as the road that visitors to Singapore know today: and along what is now the grassy median strip beside the monsoon drain, was the railway track which then ran right into the city. Many planters took the train up to Kuala Lumpur or Bangkok after a few days of rest and pleasure in Singapore.

There were two airfields at the north of the island, a third in the west and a fourth, which was the civil airport, at Kallang, 4 km from the city and built, like so much of Singapore, on reclaimed land. (Payar Lebar Airport, the main international airport until Changi was opened, replaced Kallang after the war.)

Almost nothing was paid for by Europeans in cash. Everything was bought on the so-called chit system (*chitty* being the Hindi word for note or message), from drinks to prostitutes, to a horse to one's clothes.

However crass or modest the background of a European, particularly the British, however stupid he might be, he was at the top of the colony's rigid caste system that many of them took into captivity with them, and he lived like a prince. An early commentator on colonial Singapore, Roland Braddell, advised new arrivals to observe the advice he had received from his own father: 'If you want to be happy in Singapore, don't admit that you're living in an oriental country: live as nearly as possible as you would in Europe.'

At the other end of the social scale were the Eurasians of whom there were a conservative 12 000 before they were joined by others fleeing ahead of the Japanese from up-country. The children of European men and Asian girls (very seldom the other way round), they fitted nowhere. The Europeans referred to them disparagingly as *stengahs*, the same word, meaning 'half', that they used for a small whisky and soda.

On the other hand, Europeans could and often did, have a Eurasian as a mistress. But the rules were quite clear. If you had a Eurasian mistress, you kept her well away from the other Europeans (Eurasians were of course barred from the four major clubs); and if you married one, you were immediately ostracised. Many European men happily paid this price to marry the Eurasian girls they had fallen in love with, some of whom were extremely beautiful; but there were also many heart-rending scenes when these women, sometimes looking as European as the men who had enjoyed them, were abandoned to their fate and to the Japanese when they were discarded like unwanted pets and the European women sailed away to safety.

Even in gaol, the European could take it for granted that he would not be expected to serve his time in the same cell or even the same wing as an Asian or Eurasian. Right up to the start of World War II, new arrivals, particularly the British and Australians, were being cautioned in a booklet they were given, not to hit or kick their rickshaw drivers in the street.

The city of Singapore lay at the southern end of the island, while the naval base was at the north and the great cantonment of Changi, a complex of barracks and defence sites as well as the city

15

gaol, was at the east. Changi included the big guns which were intended to defend the eastern approaches to the Johore Strait against attack from the sea.

It takes only a glance at a map to see why Singapore was so vulnerable to attack from the north. The whole island was less than 600 sq km in area, 40 km wide at its widest and never more than 21 km from north to south, so that the whole of it was within range of artillery fire from the mainland of Malaya just across the narrow Strait of Johore.

The strait was spanned by a broad causeway, 1100 m long, that carried a two-lane road, the railway track and, vitally for Singapore, a water main because, except for rain catchment, all the island's water came (as it still does) from Johore. At the northern end of the causeway was the capital of Johore State, Johore Bahru, a rather grubby town dominated by the administrative buildings and the Sultan's enormous palace.

To the west of the causeway, the strait was between 600 and 2000 m wide and at high water could be navigated by ships of medium draught; but east of the causeway it was much wider, almost 5000 m wide at the opening into the South China Sea, and it was navigable by the largest ships afloat. It was on this eastern side that the naval base had been built.

Topographically, the island was fairly flat and of the only three small hills of any significance, the highest, Bukit Timah, rose to less than 200 m. Bukit Timah was roughly mid-way between the city and the causeway.

The Australians of 22nd Brigade, newly arrived and trying to familiarise themselves with this steaming, jungle-covered island, saw that it could be divided for convenience into three main regions which could have great relevance if they were ever forced to fight across it.

Looking at Singapore from west to east, left to right, the western third had a landscape that was of ridges and vales, the ridges rising to only about 110 m. This region contained two of the island's main rivers, the Kranji, flowing into Johore Strait, and the Jurong flowing southwards into the Singapore Strait. Both would play a prominent role in the fighting.

The centre of the island was more hilly, with rounded granite hills that had proved resistant to weathering and so still stood out above the remainder of the island. These hills, or *bukits*, of which the highest was Bukit Timah, would also be tactically important. Most of Singapore's rivers rose in these central hills and flowed eastwards and small river valleys had been dammed to form the three reservoirs, fed by the pipeline, that supplied Singapore with its water.

The third part of the island, in the east, was very sandy and flat, seldom rising more than 15 m above sea level. Smaller rivers flowed to the coast and their mouths were mangrove swamps.

Indeed around most of the coast, there was mangrove linked by small rivers and streams that flooded at high tide. The most inaccessible part of the island was the north-west, which consisted mainly of dark mangrove swamps, criss-crossed by more creeks and rivers and by its very nature poorly served by roads. It was this part of the island, however, which was on the narrowest part of the strait, barely 600 m from Johore on the other side, and it was an area that the Australians would come to know uncomfortably well.

There were places on the island that then, as now, were completely uninhabited, such as the forest reserve and water catchment areas in the centre, and the large marshy regions in the mouths of the rivers which spread out along the coast. Inland there were rubber plantations, small farms producing fruit, vegetables and orchids, and everywhere the jungle.

Many of the Malays still lived in traditional *kampongs*, Malay villages of clusters of rectangular wooden houses raised off the ground on stilts and roofed with *attap*, a thatch of palm leaves. Already many of the *kampongs*, so colourful in Malaya, were degenerating into huddles of shacks made from corrugated iron and old planks, where Malays, Indians and Chinese lived side by side united by nothing but their poverty.

Singapore is less than 130 km north of the equator, so the sun is always high in the sky and the temperature rises to about 26°C every day all through the year. Combined with the high humidity and the rain that falls every month, it is extremely ennervating and the Australians disliked it intensely.

In most months 150 mm of rain fall and in the two monsoon seasons, one from the north-east, the other from the south-west, this rainfall increases. Between April and November, the winds known as *sumatras* blow from the direction of Sumatra and cause much damage every year.

The first hours or so of the day are the kindest, before the full heat of the sun is felt and when a sudden blinding rain squall brings only the sweet smell of new rain on warm earth.

For the Australians, many of them city dwellers all their lives, the creatures on the island were only slightly easier to take than the awful climate. The primary forest formed a canopy 20 m above the ground, and they had pointed out to them and promptly forgot the wild breadfruit and mango and nutmeg and the strange trees bearing their fruit and flowers so high above the ground that botanists in the Botanic Gardens trained *beroc* monkeys to climb the trees and bring them down.

The primary forest was surprisingly accessible, but on the banks of the rivers and in clearings where sunlight reached the ground, secondary forest (the result of clearance that has been allowed to grow back again) was much more impenetrable. Worst of all were the saltwater mangrove swamps on the shore, regularly flooded by the tide that made troop movements almost impossible.

The men learned that most snakes were non-poisonous, except for an unpleasant creature called a spitting cobra which had a partiality for cultivated gardens and people; but the Australians couldn't find much enthusiasm for the 8 m pythons that may not have been poisonous but which did nothing to improve exercises in the jungle.

Giant frogs growing up to 22 cm in length and the Malayan bull-frog whose deafening call kept them awake after heavy rain, added a new dimension to the already frightening eeriness of the jungle; and everywhere the crickets and grasshoppers shattered the peace, sometimes stopping their din simultaneously, as though all were holding their breath waiting for some hidden creature to come out of the jungle.

Scorpions and giant centipedes, huge huntsman spiders that ate cockroaches and jumping spiders that leaped on them in their worst dreams, all added an extra dimension to their initiation, as did hornets which they were assured could kill a cow with their stings and the fireflies which the Malays kept in little round cages and wore in place of jewelry at night before always setting them free.

To their relief, there were no tigers in spite of the stories (which were true) that only eighty years before they were killing at least one person every day. The last one known to live on the island was seen, and of course shot and presumably skinned, in 1932, but they had been known to swim across to the island from Johore long after that.

Instead they only saw squirrels and tree shrews, native rats and monkeys, and everywhere the little chichaks, the tiny lizards that walked upside down on the ceilings of every Singapore home.

To men who had never before been out of Sydney, it was a strange and unsettling experience. If they found some of Singapore's fauna hard to come to terms with, the Australians were even more perplexed by what they saw as quite unrealistic behaviour by most of the humans in the colony.

If the passing of World War I with scarcely a whimper apart from a mutiny by Indian troops about to embark for Hong Kong (52 of the Indians were killed outright by a force of British soldiers and Russian, French and Japanese sailors who happened to be in port), had instilled a sense of security in everyone, it was as nothing compared with the effect that the completion of the naval base had.

People looked at the base and at the enormous guns on the island and felt safe. For all the criticism that followed the defeat of Singapore almost nobody on the island would have thought in mid-1941 that money spent on defences was worthwhile. They were too busy themselves making money, enjoying their idyllic social life and content in the knowledge that if ever trouble did arise, they would simply climb aboard the next P & O boat and sail away to safety.

In any case there was no enemy worth the cost of installing elaborate defences, the critics argued. The Japanese were a poor sort of people who couldn't fly aeroplanes and fought with swords. ('They're slit-eyed so they can't see in the dark,' they joked over their gin slings.) And Brooke-Popham added to the nonsense by saying they were neither air-minded nor properly trained.

There were several half-hearted attempts to get ARP off the ground, but it was difficult to get people interested when there was no sign of an enemy within a hundred miles, and the armed services and civil administration both kept insisting that there was no danger. Their propaganda machines continued to churn out stories that were so far removed from the truth that it was farcical, but there was no one to know better.

When the strength of the Air Force was at about its lowest and Air Force chiefs were clamouring for the aircraft that were Singapore and Malaya's only hope now that the British fleet could not be relied on, this dispatch was sent to a London newspaper at the instigation of the government publicists. It was published the following day:

I bring you good news — there is no need to worry about the strength of the Air Force that will oppose the Japanese should they send their army and navy southward...The Air Force is on the spot, and is waiting for the enemy — clouds of bombers and fighters are hidden in the jungle, and are ready to move out on to camouflaged tarmacs of our secret landing fields and roar into action at the first move of the Japanese towards this part of the world...The planes...consist of the most modern planes Britain, Australia and America are producing.

Whoever this nonsense was supposed to confuse it can hardly have been the Japanese whose intelligence was known to be excellent. The only people who were misled were the civilians whose complacency was increased still further when the article was reproduced in the *Straits Times*.

This complacency reached such a point that an American girl returning to the island after a visit to the United States, where patriotism was giving a new momentum to preparations for war, told a radio reporter that, 'There is so much flag-waving and war spirit and talk about the war at home, that it's a relief to get back to the peace and quiet and indifference of Singapore'.

For the Europeans in Singapore, civilians and servicemen, it was exactly like living in a big garrison town during peace-time manoeuvres. There was work to be done during the day, but in the evening the social life went on as it had for a century. There was dancing every night and a tea dance twice a week; drink was unrestricted and as the brigade had seen as it landed from the *Queen Mary*, people dressed for dinner and lived in a world that had no place for horrid little yellow people who wouldn't dare to take on the might of the British Empire.

Every Sunday they bathed, either at the Tanglin Club or the Swimming Club, or on the blindingly white beaches facing Johore on which not a single pill-box or roll of barbed wire marred the unbroken expanse of sand.

Life, never overly arduous for Europeans apart from the climate and periods of intense boredom, was made doubly comfortable by the army of servants that most of them had. You phoned home from your club to say that an unexpected dozen guests would be coming for dinner that evening and you could be sure that by the time you got back, the meal would be ready at precisely the time you ordered it and with a servant standing there with your favourite pre-dinner drink as you opened the door.

It was only too easy in such an environment to convince yourself that the occasional obtrusive rumours and rumblings about war and invasion were somebody else's problem, not your own. And how could the Japanese be a threat, they asked one another rhetorically, when they were still being supplied with iron ore, wolfram and manganese, the metals of war, by Menzies in Australia and by the British? There was no talk then of the opprobrious sobriquet 'Pig-iron Bob' that would stick with Menzies for the rest of his life.

There were some on the island, of course, who were concerned. Journalists knew what the true situation was about the lack of preparedness and raged at their helplessness to tell the people the truth. If they ever brought the subject up at parties with people they didn't know, they stood the likelihood of being ridiculed or shouted down for being unpatriotic. And those coming back from China and Japan, who had sensed the growing excitement among the Japanese, knew that something was afoot.

The Auxiliary Fire Service did what training it could, but it had little equipment and not even any helmets until a consignment of helmets destined for Thailand was diverted from one of the go-downs. For the rest of the war, the Singapore AFS went about its duties in helmets that were identical to the jerry-cans worn by the Germans in World War I, complete with the spike.

The ARP held lectures, but the general level at which they were pitched was typified by a meeting that George Hammonds, assistant editor of the *Malay Tribune*, encountered during a talk by an RAF officer. This man had said, in all seriousness, that there was no need for ARP stations to be manned at night because the Japanese pilots were myopic and couldn't fly in the dark.

Face to Face
with the Jungle

Nobody viewed the complacency and apathy of most of the Europeans with as much cynicism as Major-General Gordon Bennett. Although he was a divisional commander, Bennett was in Singapore with only one of his brigades. He had left the 23rd and 27th behind and soon after he arrived on the island, he was told that the 23rd was to be moved to the Northern Territory and that two of its battalions would be sent to Timor and Ambon; and that the 27th would probably go to Alice Springs.

He was likely therefore to have two thirds of his divisions scattered far and wide and one third with him in Malaya — a highly unsatisfactory state of affairs for any commander and for the morale of the men. It was also undesirable for the Brigade Commander of the 22nd, Brigadier H. B. Taylor who found that his divisional commander had almost no troops to command except his own brigade.

Bennett was given the choice of staying as area commander in Malaya, or returning to Australia to command the larger part of his division. Without hesitation he chose to stay where he was.

Everything to do with the 8th Division was coloured by the personality of this acerbic and controversial commander. Most of his fellow officers found him a difficult man to get on with. He could be cruelly sarcastic and abrasive, he was often rude and tactless and he made little effort to curb his tongue or to disguise his views of anyone who disagreed with him.

This frequently included people senior to himself, regardless of whether they were British, Australian or Indian. The Indians' conduct on the battlefield and tactics frequently displeased him.

For Sir Thomas Blamey, the Australian Commander-in-Chief, he nursed a formidable and entirely mutual dislike which had endured over the years; and not surprisingly he was often at loggerheads with his colleagues, especially those who believed that officers should speak about their superiors only in hushed tones of awe.

One of Bennett's most unfortunate disagreements was with Brigadier Taylor of his own 22nd Brigade. Taylor was just as outspoken and dogmatic as Bennett and the two men quickly found that they shared a cordial dislike of one another. Under normal conditions, if the Division had been at full strength, they would have found it easier to avoid each other, but Bennett did not have three infantry brigades and an assortment of other units. There was only one brigade, but a divisional commander and a brigadier, so that Bennett had almost nothing else to command.

During an exercise to test the men's training, a sharp disagreement flared up between the two men about the timing of the exercise. The fierceness of it was quite disproportionate to whatever the argument was about and it exposed publicly for the first time the very raw nerve. With help from other officers it was patched up, but for the rest of the campaign the two men treated each other very warily and there were several occasions when Taylor's claims to have misunderstood Bennett's orders looked to Bennett more like wilful disobedience or insolence.

But Bennett, who was above all else an imaginative and brave soldier, recognised Taylor's skills as a commander. It was not until the last days of fighting on Singapore that he relieved him of his command after Taylor, exhausted by nights without sleep, collapsed.

Many officers thought that Bennett had a chip on his shoulder in which they were undoubtedly right; and that because he was only a part-time soldier (he had been a businessman between the wars), he must be untrained in the theory of modern warfare and therefore unfit to hold such high command. And in this they were quite wrong.

What they chose to overlook was that during World War I, he was considered so outstanding an officer that he was a brigadier-general by the time he was twenty-nine (the youngest ever in the AIF); and that between the wars, when he was in business in Sydney, he also commanded the 2nd Division of the AMF. He was tough and aggressive and absolutely fearless and in the First War he had been decorated twice and mentioned in dispatches eight times.

Bennett reserved his most strident criticism for slackness and lack of preparation wherever he found it. He remembered all too well the disasters which had followed at Gallipoli and in France when untrained troops had been committed to battles for which they were unprepared and he was determined that his men would not fall into the same trap in the jungles of Malaya and Singapore.

To achieve this and to ward off the boredom that he knew would be one of the worst enemies they had to contend with, he trained his men hard and ceaselessly. If he made too many enemies along his way, he at least ensured that when his men were put to the test, they were the best trained unit in Australia and the troops most feared and respected by the Japanese.

Before nightfall on the day they disembarked from the *Queen Mary*, the brigade had been packed into railway carriages and were on their way to Port Dickson on the west coast of the Malay Peninsula and to Seramban, 32 km inland and 330 km from Singapore. He located his own headquarters at Kuala Lumpur.

The Australians came under the operational control of the GOC Malaya, but Bennett was given a remarkably large degree of freedom of action, considering how small was the force that he actually commanded. The division had to retain its identity as an Australian force, it was always to operate together and not split up into parts, particularly by being used to relieve other units, and if the GOC insisted on using the Australians in a way that Bennett did not approve of, he was to comply but complain immediately to Army Headquarters in Melbourne.

It was a situation that would have caused friction with men of much greater sensitivity and tact than Bennett, and inevitably it caused friction in Malaya.

To General Percival who arrived as GOC shortly after the brigade, Bennett became a frequent source of annoyance, although he recognised and respected his skills as a commander. Bennett was given direct access to Army Minister Percy Spender in Australia to avoid delays in communication and to ensure that the Australian troops were never unfairly imposed on by their British commander.

Initially, it would be more accurate to say that Bennett assumed this right without actually being formally given it and General Blamey resented it as keenly as Percival. He ordered him to stop communicating with Spender and it was left to Spender himself to have the Military Board's decision reversed. Spender wrote a personal letter to Bennett assuring him that he was to continue to have the right of direct access. Bennett was formally appointed GOC AIF Malaya shortly afterwards.

Bennett put his men to training in the steamy heat and lush tropical vegetation at the first opportunity. He taught them to deal with the jungle on its own terms. His constant theme was that the jungle was an ally of those who understood it and an enemy of those who didn't.

He explained to them how the Japanese had perfected their tactics of infiltrating between posts so that they suddenly appeared in the middle of an enemy position; or if that was too difficult of moving small parties on to a flank from where they could threaten either the flank itself or the rear of the position they were attacking.

When they used these tactics against inexperienced men, the effect was likely to be so frightening that the defenders often turned tail and fled. The only way to counter these tactics, Bennett told them repeatedly, was not to be intimidated, not to look on the Japanese as some kind of super-race but as a brave, resourceful enemy, and to send out strong counter-attacking parties.

Every individual Australian in the forward zone, he urged, should accept the task of killing at least ten Japanese.

Brigadier Taylor, who shared Bennett's enthusiasm for hard training, placed great emphasis on every man being able to use his weapons for personal defence. The likelihood of meeting the enemy suddenly and at close quarters in the jungle, called for a high degree of self-reliance and speed was vital. Those who didn't react instinctively would surely die.

The infantry practised bayonet assaults and snap shooting day after day until by the time they finally came face to face with the Japanese, they were by far the most effective defenders.

Major C. G. W. Anderson had campaigned in East Africa in World War I against the German-led Askari and he possessed valuable jungle experience. Taylor now gave him the responsibility for training the Australians in jungle warfare. Anderson later won the Victoria Cross in Malaya (one of only two awarded in the campaign, the other going to Brigadier A. E. Cumming of the Indian Army).

The Australians learned that they could never take the good-will or trustworthiness of the local people for granted and that in an emergency the Chinese were much less likely to betray them than the Malays, which proved to be the case. And they learned how to move in the jungle without getting lost. The only antidote to jungle fear, which could be as terrifying as any enemy, Anderson told them, was jungle lore which removed the mystery. Most sentries in the eerieness of the jungle at night were far more frightened by their own imaginations than anything else.

Bennett largely ignored the standard training manuals on jungle warfare — 'pompous, heavy and platitudinous', he called them — and instead introduced his men to Sakai Aboriginal tribesmen who tried, without much success, to teach the heavy-footed Australians how to move easily, silently and fast through the jungle. The heat, the frequency and suddenness of the torrential downpours of rain, the swamps, rivers and other obstacles, all made troop movement exhausting and difficult and for the first weeks they suffered badly from cramp and fatigue and an array of skin disorders.

Salt cured much of the cramp and weariness and the doctors sorted out most of the skin problems after a while. If his men still grumbled at the rigorous training they were being put through, they never doubted that Bennett's concern was only to see that they became the match of the Japanese in the jungle.

What Bennett achieved, and Percival, for example, never could, was to make them proud to be Australian soldiers and to be commanded by him. With the single proud exception of 2nd Argyll and Sutherland Highlanders, who arrived in Malaya as a part of the 12th Indian Brigade, no other unit trained with the intensity of the Australians.

Local planters thought that the Australians were crazy to attempt so much hard physical training in the tropical heat and in time the Australians were happy to put aside their early contempt of the siesta and adopted the custom themselves.

Percival found that he was being continually annoyed by Bennett, particularly over the issue of the Australian's access to his minister. This usually occurred when Percival refused to give Bennett something he wanted for his men or when he thought that they were being asked to perform tasks that were not in the best interests of Australia.

Matters came to a head when Bennett was ordered by the Governor, Sir Shenton Thomas, to use his men to break a strike of plantation workers who were demanding more money. He refused, saying that it was contrary to the interests of the Australian government that its forces should be used as strike-breakers against workers in their own country.

Percival intervened and ordered Bennett to obey the Governor, saying that it was a legal order that he could not refuse. But Bennett was adamant. Immediately after this meeting with Percival, he contacted the Australian government which in turn dispatched a signal confirming that it endorsed Bennett's stand. Australians were not to be used for this purpose. To the men in the ranks, this unswerving concern for their rights made Bennett a popular commander but the incident did nothing to improve the luke-warm relationship between the two generals.

The Australian leaders in the field were very concerned throughout the campaign that the reinforcements being sent out to Malaya were so poorly trained. The training depots in Australia were notoriously inefficient and ineffectual, mainly, it seems, because they skipped elementary training and hurried on to more interesting technical work before the men were ready for it.

Those who were sent on to the Middle East were as poorly trained, but there at least the AIF had excellent reinforcement depots where they could be retrained when they arrived. Malayan Command had no such facilities. When one large batch arrived in October, for example, the best that any of the unit commanders could say about them was that their training had been bad and their discipline was worse.

Training of quite another kind was under way at the same time to train experienced men in the art of guerilla tactics and to stay behind enemy lines. In mid-1940 the British had formed a number of commando units to raid German occupied territories in Europe. Later that same year, a group of instructors were sent to Australia to train what were known as the Independent Companies. They followed the procedures that had been developed in Britain using regular officers with special skills such as exploring, mountaineering and demolition. The training in Australia was carried out in the rugged national park at Wilson's Promontory in southern Victoria and in February 1941, the innocuously named 'No. 7 Infantry Training Centre' was established. Every six weeks, the centre turned out enough officers and NCOs to start one Australian and one New Zealand Independent Company.

In August that year, Lieutenant-Colonel Spencer Chapman, a

former schoolmaster and later the best-selling author of *The Jungle is Neutral*, was sent to Singapore to instruct the Allies in bush warfare. Chapman had been one of the instigators of the Independent Companies and he taught men, as he put it, 'to blow up everything from battleships to brigadiers', and then how to get back safely to base in any country by day or night. The men learned how to live off the country and memorise routes and how to escape if they were caught by the enemy.

At a more prosaic level, the 8th Division from its commander downwards was now being subjected to an ordeal that Australian troops had rarely encountered before. Always in the past they had volunteered to go to the front and had been sent there briskly. The 8th Division had enlisted like the others in the full expectation that this would happen. They had joined up in the wave of patriotism and enthusiasm that had followed the fall of France and then been kept alight by the Army's recruiting officers.

Instead of going straight to the front, however, the men of 8th Division found themselves scattered far and wide on garrison duties which had never been contemplated by officers or men when they had signed on.

At least the men of 22nd Brigade were serving overseas and presumably would one day encounter a real enemy, but they too came to resent the boredom and frustration and the debilitating climate that sapped their energy and pushed their patience to the limit.

Their mood was not improved by throw-away remarks by wives and girl-friends at home who wrote jokingly about the exotic lives that the soldiers were living which they were reading about in the press. If the wife or girl-friend was then foolish enough to add, equally in jest, that they knew how to have a good time as well, it was often the last straw for these angry and frustrated men.

They referred to themselves sarcastically as 'Menzies's glamour boys' and when a newsreel showing the Prime Minister inspecting Australians came on the screen at Seramban, there was a chorus of hoots and boos for the man whom they saw as being directly responsible for their miserable predicament. To the officers and men from other nations who were in the cinema it was written down as just another curious trait of the Australians, that they should boo their own Prime Minister inspecting their own comrades-in-arms!

In fact, one of Bennett's greatest achievements was in keeping up the morale of his men in the long months of boredom from the time when they arrived in Malaya until they first contacted the enemy nearly eleven months later. He also established leave and recreation clubs in Kuala Lumpur and in Singapore where the building was donated by a grateful resident of the city and turned into the Anzac Club. Organised and financed by the Australian Comforts Fund, it was staffed largely by volunteer Australian and New Zealand women living in Singapore.

There were ugly incidents in Singapore as well as in Kuala Lumpur between Australians on leave and British, especially the British Military Police. When Bennett was told that his men had been provoked — which was only partly true — he arranged with Generals Percival and Heath of III Indian Army Corps that in future AIF discipline would be maintained only by Australian Military Police.

This, of course, only increased the provocation and the British enjoyed some mild revenge after one of Percival's less successful ideas for easing the tension. The British were issued with Australian slouch hats, the most visible difference in their uniforms, so that they were hard to tell apart. The consequence of this was that many of the misdoings of the British were blamed on the Australians who were still assumed by most civilians to be the only people wearing slouch hats.

But when Percival said that Australians on leave in Singapore should pay for the Army vehicles that ferried them around, as the British were having to do, Bennett refused to even consider it. 'The least the Australian government can do for them,' he told Percival bluntly and that was the end of the matter.

There was one incident, at about the time of the strike-breaking episode, which involved Australians and which could have had far more serious repercussions. On 26 May 1941, two junior Australian officers crossed the frontier from Malaya into Thailand. Whether they were there with the knowledge of the defence forces to spy out the land, or had simply been careless as the official statement insisted, is not clear, but they were promptly arrested.

It would have been a very minor matter normally, but at that time it had the gravest possibilities for it could easily have been seized on by the Japanese as an excuse for entering Thailand on the grounds that Thai neutrality had been violated. The incident blew over, but not before news of it leaked out to be used by Japanese propagandists. When the time came for them to enter Thailand, the Japanese were not in need of such trivial excuses.

During the three months that followed the arrival of the 22nd Brigade, there were two important staff changes. Air Vice-Marshal C. W. H. Pulford arrived to take over command of the Air Force as Air Officer Commanding Far East Command and much more significantly, Lieutenant-General A. E. Percival arrived to replace General Bond as General Officer Commanding Malaya. At about the same time Lieutenant-General Sir Lewis Heath and the Headquarters of III Indian Corps also arrived.

The man who would pit his wits against the Japanese army seemed an unlikely choice. Lieutenant-General Arthur Percival had been Chief of Staff in Malaya before being promoted to Commander-in-Chief. His main claim for the top job was that in 1937 as a staff officer in Malaya, he had prepared an appreciation and a plan of attack on Singapore from the point of view of the Japanese that challenged all the existing strategical assumptions about Malaya.

In particular, Percival believed that it was quite wrong and dangerously wishful thinking to assume that the British Fleet would arrive within sixty days of the outbreak of war with Japan (which was then all that Admiralty said that it required) and that its arrival would automatically avert the danger of Singapore being captured. He challenged too the old assumption that danger would only come from the sea.

Instead he outlined a form of attack on Malaya which involved the Japanese seizing airfields in southern Thailand and northern Malaya before capturing Singapore itself. Percival's conclusion was that the defence of northern Malaya and of Johore was of far greater importance than had been thought until then, and that strong reinforcements were urgently needed.

His reasoning was so well thought out and presented that it was accepted by the Chiefs of Staff in London. It was so prophetic that it made it all the more bewildering when he turned out to be ineffectual in preparing these defences when the fate of Singapore was put in his hands.

Unusually Percival had graduated at both the Army and the Naval staff colleges and he had shown himself to be a first-rate staff officer. Throughout his career he had been thought of as an unassuming and considerate officer, but as events would prove so disastrously, he had neither the imagination, the drive nor the ruthlessness that were needed by a commander in the situation that developed in Malaya and Singapore.

A tall, rather spare Englishman, he was unimposing in appearance and with his two protruding front teeth, flushed cheeks and little moustache, he looked rather like a rabbit. More importantly and undesirably, he was also almost entirely lacking in charisma so that he was nearly as unknown to his troops at the end of the war as he was at the beginning. Least of all was he ever a match for his Japanese opponent, either as a tactician or an inspiration to his men.

Percival has subsequently been severely criticised for his disposition of his troops which the Australian official historian described as being 'fundamentally unsound'. But in spite of this, he had an impossible task from the start.

His main objective in Malaya was never to prevent the peninsula from falling into Japanese hands (which from the beginning had been accepted as an impossible demand) but rather to save the fortress of Singapore and the naval base until reinforcements arrived. That involved not only the defence of the island itself if it came under attack, but also the denial to the Japanese for as long as possible of all the numerous airfields which the Air Force had scattered around Malaya without consultation with the Army as to how they were to be defended. From any one of them, the Japanese, if they got possession of them, could bomb Singapore at will.

It was for this reason that the entire defence of Singapore had been formulated around the assumption that in the absence of a firm guarantee that the Navy would be available, the key to the entire defence of Singapore would be an air force strong enough to inflict crippling losses on an invading convoy. Such an air force was never present in anything approaching the numbers of aircraft that were required.

The Army on the other hand, still had to be deployed over a very wide area, largely to protect all these airfields and to cover all the likely landing places which the Japanese might use. The Allied intelligence network had given no hint of the decision that had been reached in Tokyo.

It could be in the Mersing area, or they might advance on the Kra

Isthmus and advance down the coast; they might choose Kota Bharu and seize the three airfields there or go to Kuantan where there was another airfield; or even, unlikely as it seemed, they might go straight to Singapore and make a landing on the island.

Every one of these was an option and Percival believed that he had to scatter his forces to try to handle each one of them. It was inevitable with this strategy that wherever the enemy made his initial attack, he was going to be superior in numbers to the defenders. If the monsoon rains were falling, the roads would be in such poor condition that they would be unable to carry a large relieving force; and if the Japanese gained an early success, the Allied reserves would be drawn into the battle very gradually because of poor communications, allowing the enemy to pick them off piecemeal.

The repeated requests that Percival had made for reinforcements and more aircraft still fell on deaf ears and he had little option but to make the best of what he had. But even allowing for this, some of his decisions appear surprising to say the least.

He allotted to the defence of the whole of Malaya north of Johore and Malacca — about nine-tenths of a country bigger than England — two weak divisions of inexperienced Indian troops from III Indian Corps. These divisions were not even up to strength in numbers, for there were only two brigades instead of the normal establishment of three.

The AIF was allotted the task of defending Johore and Malacca, the two states nearest Singapore, which put their front line less than 250 km from the island. Their area of responsibility extended right back to and included the causeway itself. Whatever the value of having this tough line of defence behind the Indians, it effectively kept the best troops in Malaya out of combat until nine-tenths of the country had fallen.

The quality of the Indian troops, who had the responsibility of defending most of Malaya, was disproportionate even to their numbers, as it was throughout the Indian Army. Field-Marshal Sir Claude Auchinleck, then a Major-General, had recently described it as 'showing a tendency to fall behind the forces of such minor states as Egypt, Iraq and Afghanistan. Judged by modern standards, the army in India is relatively immobile and under-armed and unfit to take the field against land or air forces equipped with up to date weapons.'

Traditionally the Indian Army was predominantly led by British officers who outnumbered the Indian officers by more than five to one. Many of the potential British officers for the rapidly expanding Indian Army, however, had volunteered to go to Europe or the Middle East as soon as war broke out against Germany and there were not enough of them to meet the needs of the new, expanding Indian army.

The ranks were drawn largely from illiterates who came with a multiplicity of races, castes, creeds and languages. The common language of the Army was Urdu which was foreign to many of them. New recruits needed much longer to train in India than in more advanced countries and even the normal training period was not now available to them.

As the Indian Army tended to curb rather than stimulate the nationalistic hopes of most young Indians, the recruits tended to give their loyalty to leaders who could win their respect by the strength of their personal character rather than the cause for which they were supposed to be fighting. The European officers achieved this much more effectively than other Indians.

In spite of this, many of the British officers who were volunteering were not of the traditional calibre, and many did not speak even a smattering of Urdu. Before the war the speaking of some Urdu had been a pre-requisite.

Indian regiments were a part of the British Army and another tradition was that the Indian brigades were bolstered by the addition of a British battalion in the ratio of one British battalion to two Indian ones. Again there were not enough British battalions to leaven these Indian brigades because the Indian army was expanding so fast.

In Malaya this need not have been a problem. Of the six Indian brigades in Malaya Command, only three contained a British battalion which Percival knew was essential if the Indians were to give of their best. But there were three regular British battalions on Singapore Island, relegated to the fortress, even though the chance of a landing there was slight. Why Percival did not send them to the north has never been made clear.

Instead, when the battle started, these illiterate, untrained, dissatisfied Indians, homesick, bored and depressed, who had been kept for much of the time by their officers in the perpetual half-light of the rubber plantations, became the first line of defence against some of the best-trained, most fanatical troops in the world.

By 7 December 1941, on the very eve of battle, the Allied forces' strength was still far short of what had been agreed was needed. Indeed it was short by 17 infantry battalions, 4 light anti-aircraft regiments and 2 tank regiments. There was not a single tank in the whole of Malaya although they had been requested for four years and were put to devastating use by the Japanese.

There were few armoured cars, insufficient anti-tank rifles, and a serious shortage of mobile anti-aircraft weapons. Even excluding the Indian troops, throughout the whole command there were not only shortages of equipment but defects in quality and efficiency. As the Australian official historian wrote, 'A severe shortage existed of experienced officers to administer the forces, train them and provide dependable leadership in battle; and of experienced men to leaven the rank and file.'

Or as a senior Australian officer put it more graphically, 'The quality went quickly from cream to skim milk.'

Percival's total strength was 88 600 men, but the great majority of these were support and base troops and not fighting soldiers. There were only 19 000 British and 15 200 Australians and the rest, more than 53 000, were Indians or locally enlisted volunteers, half-trained for the most part and with no knowledge of jungle warfare.

Against them the Japanese put 125 000 men, many of them blooded in China and trained in jungle warfare. They were superior in man-power, they had an overwhelming advantage in tanks and superiority on the sea and in the air.

The Japanese had made their preparations for the assault on South-East Asia with meticulous care. It was a masterpiece of strategic planning which required, if it were to succeed, split-second timing, complicated lines of communication to maintain the various units that would be fighting on several fronts simultaneously and of course a formidable fighting machine. They had it all.

For the capture of Malaya and Singapore, the Japanese planners allowed just one hundred days and in the event, they needed only seventy — a little more than two months — to achieve all their goals and 120 000 Allied prisoners besides.

A Most Dangerous Enemy

The Supreme Commander of all Japanese military operations in the region south of Japan was Field Marshal Count Hisaichi Terauchi, a member of one of Japan's most distinguished military families; and the force entrusted with the task of subduing Malaya and Singapore was the XXV Army of Lieutenant-General Tomoyuki Yamashita.

Yamashita, the man who would pit his wits against Arthur Percival, was an officer with extensive experience as a commander, although little on the battle-field. This similarity with Percival was all that the two men had in common.

A big, heavy man who gave the deceptive appearance of being almost mild, Yamashita was in fact aggressive and very ambitious. He had headed the Japanese military missions sent to Germany and Italy to study their methods of waging war and had become one of Japan's most respected tacticians. He also possessed a personality that was an inspiration to his men.

Ever since the visit to Singapore by Tokyo's planning chief, Tanikawa, in September 1940, there had been no question that the attack would be made from any direction but the north. With sea and air co-operation, Yamashita's main strength would land near the frontier of Thailand and Malaya on the Kra Isthmus, actually in Thai territory, and spread out across the peninsula and down through Malaya.

Meanwhile another landing would be made simultaneously near Kota Bharu on the Malayan coast and these troops would push down to the southern end of the peninsula until they were positioned across the strait from Singapore from where an assault on the island itself would be launched.

Most of the Japanese conscripts came from a background that was little different from that of the Indians. They were labourers and peasants with little formal education, but who in time of peace were trained rigorously for two years and then passed into the reserve. The Japanese training was probably more exacting than that of any other in the world, particularly in hardening them to endure extremes of heat and cold, fatigue and hunger.

One observer reported that in operations in Manchuria, the troops went entirely without food for three days, in weather so cold that their water was constantly frozen in their flasks.

In 1941, however, Japan had been fighting China for four years and many veteran reservists had been recalled for a second tour of duty. They were therefore seasoned and battle-hardened soldiers.

They had an ever-present conviction that they were obligated to the Divine Emperor, to the Japanese community and to its individual members. The Japanese fully understood these obligations, but few outsiders came close to knowing what they meant. Certainly few Australians could understand why the greatest honour a Japanese soldier felt he could attain was to die for his Emperor, or why a soldier who was taken prisoner was regarded as an outcast, or why a commander whose force was defeated should, and often did, commit suicide. But combined with their training this philosophy produced well-trained, fanatical and brave fighters.

They were also skilled at amphibious operations and highly innovative. For example, they made use of bicycles when the Allies were mocking such an idea and developed them into the ideal form of mass transport on the low-grade Asian roads and jungle tracks. They were past masters at trickery, whether it was to use pyrotechnics to simulate weapon fire and divert their opponents, or calling out in English to lure their enemy out into the open.

They were expert at the laying of booby traps and they used torture routinely and savagely as a part of their normal interrogation procedure. Coupled with the fact that to most Europeans they also *looked* sinister in their drab uniforms and caps, they began with a strong psychological advantage. It was this above all that Bennett and Taylor sought to neutralise in their training.

As with the Americans, the Japanese Army and Navy each possessed their own air force, and the combined strength of the two forces was about 5000 first-line machines with adequate reserves for any immediate requirement. Percival had 158 aeroplanes of which fully a half were obsolete. And contrary to the patronising jokes being told in Singapore, the Japanese were first-rate airmen.

On the sea, Japan had a navy more powerful than the combined strength of all the other naval forces in the Pacific, even before Pearl Harbour, including 11 battleships, 10 aircraft carriers and 39 cruisers which were administratively divided into 6 fleets.

This, then, was the formidable foe that the Australians, the British and the Indians, waiting in their little pockets, under-trained, under-equipped and short of ammunition, were about to face.

In Australia Prime Minister Menzies had become increasingly disillusioned about the extent to which Australia could rely on Britain coming to the defence of Singapore. He said openly in Cabinet that Churchill had no conception of the British Dominions as separate entities and that the further they were from London, the less he even thought about it.

'It is now evident that for far too long we have readily accepted the general assurances about the defence of this area,' he said. And it was a theme that would be echoed even more publicly by John Curtin who became Prime Minister in October 1941 and who told the nation, 'I make it quite clear that Australia looks to America, free from any pangs as to our traditional links of kinship with the United Kingdom. We know the problems with which the United Kingdom is faced: we know too that Australia can go and Britain can still hold on. We are determined that Australia shall not go.'

Menzies made inquiries of his own in London and was even more concerned by what he learned. He was convinced that Churchill's pledge that if the threat of an attack on Australia by Japan eventuated, Britain would cut her losses in the Mediterranean and go at once to her aid, was empty rhetoric. Said Menzies, 'It was stressed to me that such a step would not be practicable until after the lapse of a considerable period and might not be possible even then.'

The Australian War Cabinet decided that a British suggestion that two additional Australian infantry brigades be sent to Malaya could not be considered without a complete review of Australia's manpower position. It would achieve nothing if these troops were poured into the Malayan war machine to do nothing more than delay the Japanese for a few weeks while a possibly non-existent relieving force was on the way, and Australia was left with no means of defending herself against an actual Japanese invasion.

In the end a compromise was reached and War Cabinet determined that a second brigade of Bennett's 8th Division, the 27th, should be sent to Malaya. Bennett was overjoyed when he was told that the brigade was coming back to him. It consisted of the 2/26th, 2/29th and 2/30th battalions and supporting units, the 2/26th from Queensland, the 2/29th from Victoria, and the 2/30th from New South Wales. The brigade was commanded by a relatively young brigadier, D. S. Maxwell who, like Taylor of the 22nd, was a medical doctor by profession.

The arrival of the 27th Brigade meant that the 8th Australian Division was finally released from the Command Reserve. It was a role that Bennett had never enjoyed and he had left General Percival in no doubt that if his men remained in reserve after war broke out, his force would sooner or later inevitably be broken up and sent piece-meal to relieve the Indian units. And this, as he constantly reminded Percival, was contrary to the Australian government's policy.

The division was given a definite area of responsibility in Johore and Malacca. The east coast of Johore, the most southerly state in Malaya and the state at the northern end of the causeway on to Singapore Island, was an obvious landing place for the Japanese. It offered the advantage that, if the landing was executed properly, it would allow the Japanese to cut the lines of communication of III Indian Corps which was defending northern Malaya. It would then be isolated and could be destroyed at their leisure.

As the Australians had no idea what the Japanese plans were, they had to plan for every eventuality. Bennett, like Percival on the larger scale, had to cover as many options as possible with the troops at his disposal. A major issue generally in Malaya had been whether to try to hold the beaches if the Japanese landed or to place the Allies' forces further back from the sea to defend the roads leading into the interior.

To defend the beaches would involve spreading the troops very thinly and leave nothing in reserve for a counter-attack. On the other hand, the Japanese would be most vulnerable when they were disembarking and coming ashore. On balance Brooke-Popham had been impressed by this argument and had ordered the first line of defence to be the beaches which Percival now put into effect.

Brooke-Popham never disputed that in making his decision, he was largely influenced by the assurance of the RAF that it was strong enough to stop any invasion in Malaya and would inflict on any enemy convoy losses as high as 40 per cent. However he did not change his plans when it became clear that the aircraft to do this did not exist.

Bennett established his headquarters at Johore Bahru and quickly established a very friendly rapport with Sir Ibrahim, the Sultan (like many Malayans and Indonesians he used only his given name), who offered and gave the Australians much aid.

The 22nd Brigade replaced the 12th Indian Brigade in the Mersing-Endau area where it was anticipated the Japanese were most likely to land. The 27th, which had been on Singapore Island since it arrived, was to be deployed mainly in north-western Johore, but was given battle stations that would allow it to go to the support of the 22nd in a counter-attack if the need arose. The 12th Indian Brigade became Percival's reserve.

Bennett's new role in Malaya and in the defence of Singapore encouraged him to ask for his other units to be given back to him, but he was told that they were to be kept in Australia and taken from his command altogether. Even a machine gun battalion and a pioneer battalion which he had been asking for since March were not to be sent to Malaya.

The fear of the Japanese landing at Singora, the only port of any size on the east coast of the Kra Isthmus, and across the border from Malaya in Thailand, was so real that in November 1941 Brooke-Popham pressed London again for a final decision in the question of whether he could cross the border in spite of Thailand's ostensible neutrality. It was vital, he argued, that the Allies act before the Japanese landed.

If he had possession of the town, he estimated that he would have to be in a position to repel an attack by at least one Japanese division advancing overland from Bangkok and two more coming in from the sea.

The British officers he had sent up to reconnoitre the area met their Japanese counterparts, also in plain clothes, doing the same thing, which only reinforced Brooke-Popham's view that something was in the offing.

The operation that he proposed for resisting the seizure of Singora was given the code-name MATADOR, but although it could have been critical to the defence of Malaya and Singapore,

Brooke-Popham was refused the reinforcements he wanted to put it into effect and was told moreover that for political reasons he could not anticipate any raid by going in before it actually occurred. This meant that he would need at least 36 hours which in turn meant that MATADOR would have almost no chance of succeeding.

In September 1941, Winston Churchill sent Alfred Duff Cooper, who had been his Minister of Information, out to Singapore. Duff Cooper, close friend of the abdicated King Edward VIII and of Churchill himself, was appointed to settle urgent political matters on the spot which had previously all been referred back to London. He was given the title of Resident Minister for Far Eastern Affairs and, as Chancellor of the Duchy of Lancaster, had cabinet rank.

His secondary brief was to investigate the steps being taken by the Dominion and Colonial governments in the Far East to prepare for a war with Japan. His area of responsibility extended from Malaya and Hong Kong down to Australia and New Zealand.

He proved to be the scourge of bureaucracy and red tape, pin-pointing inefficiencies and wastage with laser-like precision. Newspaper editors and most people outside government greeted him as a much needed breath of fresh air, and many public servants wished that he had never come near the place.

The Governor, Sir Shenton Thomas, in particular resented Duff Cooper's interference in the century-old operation of the bureaucracy, especially when later the minister was appointed chairman of the War Council. 'Until then,' Thomas told a friend, 'he was at least always pleasant. After that he was exactly the reverse.'

A similar minister of state had been appointed in the Middle East and had been successful in clearing many of the bottle-necks that arose when a quick political decision was needed. Australia's desire to have a voice in the conduct of affairs in the Far East was also satisfied when her Commissioner in China, V. G. Bowden, was appointed representative in Singapore. Bowden brought with him twenty-five years' experience in China and Japan. He had served with the British army in France during World War I. He played a most valuable role until he was murdered by Japanese soldiers while trying to escape from Singapore in the last days before the surrender.

Duff Cooper was known to have a formidable temper — 'when he gets into gear, his veins stand out and he looks as though he's about to have a seizure,' Churchill told Lord Moran, his doctor — but his job in Singapore most called for tact and persistence. He had both in full measure.

When Duff Cooper arrived, almost everybody told him that Japan was too weak to enter the war. Only one man, an Englishman called Sir John Sansom who was one of the greatest living authorities on Japanese art and who knew Japan intimately, told him 'gently and very sadly', as Duff Cooper recalled, that he was sure Japan would enter the war. 'After that I wasted no more time collecting the views of soldiers and civil servants.'

He did, however, continue his interviews, including a visit one day to Gordon Bennett and the AIF. He had lunch with Bennett but never made it as far as the Australian lines because he found to his astonishment that the general's headquarters were 130 km from his nearest troops.

Duff Cooper's special concern was that the rusting, Victorian administration that existed for handling Singapore's problems in London would seriously impede the island's ability to defend itself properly if ever it was seriously threatened. On the island, as Governor of a Crown Colony, the Governor's word was almost law, and Sir Shenton Thomas, a career bureaucrat all his life, was untroubled by such inconveniences as a democratically elected parliament or house of assembly. He made the rules and the people followed them.

At the London end, however, there had traditionally been four government departments directly concerned in the day-to-day administration of the island colony. Since the start of the war, two more had been added, Information and Economic Warfare. The last thing Duff Cooper wanted to see happening as a result of his appointment, was the addition of a seventh department to oversee the other six and he recommended the appointment of just one man who would have the title Commissioner General for the Far East. This man would override all other public servants and would be able to cut through red-tape in any of the Far Eastern countries where Britain ruled.

If war came, a Far Eastern War Council would come into existence, a kind of War Cabinet, for that theatre and the Commissioner General would automatically become its head. In the meantime he should prepare himself for the job by travelling continuously between the various countries.

The main obstacle to such an appointment was the shortage of men qualified to do it who would also be acceptable internationally — as Duff Cooper put it, 'who could talk with ambassadors, governors and commanders-in-chief on terms of equality, and be received by the Viceroy in India and the President in Washington'.

One man stood out in Duff Cooper's assessment and that was Robert Menzies of Australia. Duff Cooper had met and admired him and he was also out of office which made him politically acceptable. But having been Prime Minister, 'he would carry the necessary guns and would know how to use them'.

Duff Cooper discussed the matter later with Menzies in Melbourne and the Australian liked the idea, but events intervened. The Japanese came into the war even sooner than the most pessimistic had thought likely and military commanders stepped in.

On his first visit to Australia, when he put his proposal to Menzies, Duff Cooper stayed for a few nights in Canberra, 'that strangest of capitals where all is make-believe'. He wrote that he had not been sure if he would like either Australia or the Australians, but he found he liked both very much indeed, and perhaps inevitably, Australians liked him.

'I found the country far more beautiful than I had expected and the people warm-hearted, truly hospitable and tremendously alive,' he wrote.

Duff Cooper and his vivacious and remarkable wife Lady Diana — one of the handful of women who were not intimidated by Churchill — quickly made their mark in Singapore's social life, while Duff Cooper himself marvelled at the inefficiencies he found all around him.

Almost next door to his own office he found two British civil servants, one from the Ministry of Information, the other from Economic Warfare. Each had his own staff of lesser civil servants and each was doing precisely the same job as the other. The two men were on good terms, lived in the same house and showed one another everything they were doing.

Their only objection to what Duff Cooper called 'this absurd system' was that neither of them had access to any naval or military information that might have been of any use to them, so that their work was almost totally valueless. They were not officially denied this access, but the only contact they had been told they could have with the forces was through an ex-naval officer who had rejoined the service after twenty years as a magistrate in Fiji. His conception of his duties, as Duff Cooper put it, 'was to prevent anybody 'from obtaining any information whatever.'

The belief, which persisted until almost the very day the Japanese landed, that they would not attack Malaya, persisted in the face of all the evidence and all the intelligence reports. A conference presided over by Duff Cooper in the last week of September and attended by Brooke-Popham, the naval Commander-in-Chief, Sir Shenton Thomas and political advisers from Britain and Australia, reached the conclusion that the Japanese would be most unlikely to attempt any landing on Malaya during the north-east monsoon which was due to begin in October, even if Tokyo had made the decision to go to war. All the thinking was that the Japanese were concentrating their immediate future military efforts on fighting the Russians.

Nor was it only in Singapore that these optimistic estimates were being made. On his way through Manila in the Philippines, the Australian Minister for Commerce, Sir Earle Page, who had been sent to London by Menzies to emphasise the urgency of reinforcements being sent to Singapore, was assured by General MacArthur that after five years of war in China, Japan was over-extended and would have to have a long period of recuperation before she could undertake another major struggle. 'She has gone to the limits of her southward expansion,' MacArthur said adamantly.

Yet twenty-three days before the conference that Duff Cooper had presided over in Singapore, the Japanese leaders had decided that unless America agreed by 25 November to their terms (no more aid for China, no increase in British and US forces in the Far East, no interference in Indo-China and full co-operation by the US with Japan to supply her with raw materials) Japan would go to war. The Minister for War then was General Tojo and by the time that date had passed, Tojo, the most powerful hawk, had become Prime Minister while still retaining his War portfolio. Any hope of peace had gone.

All this information was being passed by Tokyo to the Japanese Embassy in Washington and intercepted by the American intelligence agencies, as they had been doing since they cracked Tokyo's codes the previous year. 'Magic', as the intercepted messages were code-named, had provided a constant stream of information, but not apparently convincing enough for MacArthur to change his view about Japanese intentions. And 'Magic' was of no help in preventing the surprise attack on Pearl Harbour.

From the end of November the pace of events stepped up. Brooke-Popham learned of an increasingly strong concentration of Japanese sea, land and air forces in southern Indo-China and the China Sea. A telegram from the British War Office warned of the imminent collapse of the Washington negotiations with the Japanese which had been dragging on fruitlessly for weeks. If this occurred, he was told, Japan could be expected to attack Thailand, the Netherlands East Indies or the Philippines.

A report arrived from Saigon warning that the Japanese intended to land in southern Thailand on 1 December and Air Headquarters were warned to be ready to support operation MATADOR at twelve hours notice. And on 5 December, Brooke-Popham was finally told that he could order MATADOR to proceed without reference to London if a Japanese landing seemed imminent or the Japanese violated any other part of Thailand.

Only days before, however, the British Chiefs of Staff had also impressed on him that if the Japanese were intending to land in southern Thailand, they would certainly use the start of MATADOR as an immediate excuse for going to war. He was therefore to be scrupulously careful in acting on his own initiative and indeed so cautiously did he proceed that he left it too late for MATADOR to be implemented at all.

On 29 November all troops away from barracks in Singapore had been ordered back at once and the Volunteers were being mobilised, the second round of readiness. It also marked the start of a major round-up of the Japanese civilians in Singapore and Malaya who had not already gone in response to clandestine messages secretly delivered by Japanese or sympathising couriers.

Less than a week later, all army leave in Australia was cancelled. The following day, soon after noon local time, a Hudson from No. 1 Squadron Royal Australian Air Force, operating out of Kota Bharu, reported sighting three transports and an escort destroyer about 130 km south of Cape Cambodia steering north-west.

Brooke-Popham was very reluctant to invoke MATADOR on the strength of this one sighting after the warning that he had been given by London as to the almost certain consequences if he did. The ship could well be a part of a force setting out to attack Thailand, or even to hug the coast round the Gulf of Thailand and come down to Malaya; but it could equally be just another move in the Japanese war of nerves and still no word had been received of an actual breakdown in the Washington talks. He decided that he would not be justified in ordering MATADOR, but put all his forces on the highest degree of readiness, and ordered the Air Force to keep contact with the Japanese ships.

But when they looked again, the Air Force could not find the Japanese. A Catalina flying boat returned to Singapore on the morning of the 7th without seeing anything because of bad weather; and a second Catalina despatched at 2.00 a.m. on the same day failed to return to base or to send any message.

In fact the invasion fleet had been despatched shortly before the first sighting and had been ordered to keep close to the coast and take advantage of the bad weather which with luck would allow it to get right across the gulf without being spotted by Allied air patrols.

The second Catalina from Singapore had by chance arrived over a part of the fleet in a small break in the cloud and it was still taking in what it saw and maintaining radio silence, when a Japanese fighter swooped down and destroyed it.

'If this enemy sea-plane had observed our convoy and reported it by wireless,' Yamashita's Chief of Staff, General Susuki, said later, 'our Malaya landing operation might have been a dismal failure.'

Finally two Hudsons did find their quarry. First an aircraft from No. 8 Australian Squadron spotted a Japanese vessel with a large number of men on deck wearing khaki; and then a second Hudson at 5.50 p.m. and only 180 km north of Kota Bharu, saw a merchant vessel and a cruiser. It was immediately fired on but escaped into the cloud. Then again at 6.48, through a gap in the dense cloud, four more Japanese ships were seen off the coast of Thailand, this time about 240 km from Kota Bharu and steaming south.

Brooke-Popham recorded that this last report did not reach him until 9.00 p.m., although official accounts vary and some put the time at sixty minutes earlier. He called a conference at the Naval Base at which he, General Percival and Admiral Sir Tom Phillips, the Commander-in-Chief Eastern Fleet were present. All three agreed that MATADOR should still not be ordered that night.

Percival argued that if the Japanese were heading for Singora, it was most unlikely that they would be forestalled by MATADOR.

He told Brooke-Popham that he considered that the other risks were so high that the operation would be basically unsound. Indeed Brooke-Popham still had no authority to order an attack on a Japanese expedition at sea until the Japanese had committed some definitely hostile act. And apparently he did not consider the firing on the Hudson or the probable shooting down of the Catalina which failed to return, as being definitely hostile acts.

The Japanese, undisturbed, sailed on down the coast and at 10.20 p.m. that same night, the first ships dropped anchor off Kota Bharu. Almost at once they were fired on from the shore and returned the fire with their heavy guns. High seas complicated the launching of the landing craft and many capsized throwing out their occupants. When they did get away from the ships' sides, they found it difficult to maintain direction. By 3.30 a.m., however, the landings were well under way.

The heavy rain, high seas and fierce fire from the defenders caused heavy losses as the Japanese tried to penetrate the barbed wire on the beach, but they stormed in, all converging on a single gap in the wire. Their discipline held and after a short and bloody exchange and hand-to-hand fighting, they surged ahead.

Opposing them were about the same number of men of the 8th Indian Brigade, but as everywhere on the peninsula, they were spread far too thinly on the ground. Even had they been well trained, they would have stood no chance.

As it was, the Japanese raced forwards and the Indians collapsed. They could hardly be blamed. Almost fresh from the streets as most of them were, they behaved as most people would if they were suddenly confronted by a horde of wildly screaming, fanatical Japanese coming straight at them with fixed bayonets. Some were so shocked they could hardly raise their weapons to defend themselves and died on the spot, some made a valiant but futile effort to fight, while others simply ran away. Of these some wandered around in the jungle for a few days before being caught and many of those who were captured later turned on their former comrades and fought alongside the Japanese.

By dawn on the 8th, seventeen sorties had been carried out by Hudsons of No. 1 Squadron RAAF against the Japanese ships and troops landing at Kota Bharu. The heavy rain and thick blanket of cloud which hung low over the sea would normally have made Kota Bharu unserviceable, but somehow the ground staff and crews continued to take off and make low-level attacks on the Japanese convoy through intense anti-aircraft fire.

They destroyed one transport which blew up, set fire to a second one which contained tanks and artillery and damaged a third. Of the squadron's ten serviceable Hudsons, two with their crews were lost, one captained by the flight lieutenant, J. C. Ramshaw, who had first located the Japanese invasion fleet. Most of the other Hudsons were damaged but by soon after first light had been repaired and were back in the air flying more sorties over the Japanese ashore.

At 7.30 Japanese bombers and fighters began making heavy attacks on Malaya's northern airfields, skilfully using only light bombs against planes and personnel so that there would be no serious damage to the surfaces of the fields. They proved to be very adept at arriving at the airfield when the defending aircraft were either taking off or landing and the accuracy of their bombing gave the lie to all the tired jokes in Singapore's clubs about short-sighted Japanese pilots. Percival was not alone when he said later that this skill in the air 'came as an unpleasant surprise'.

It should not have done, because intelligence reports had already given details of the performance of the Zero fighters which had been fitted with auxiliary fuel tanks to give them greater range.

At the same time as the landings were being made at Kota Bharu, the two main landings were taking place further north at Singora and Patani in Thailand by the 5th Japanese Division. These encountered almost no opposition. Another smaller landing was made north of Singora by men whose task was to secure the single-line railway between Bangkok and the frontier with Malaya.

In these first landings, in addition to the 5500 troops who had fought their way ashore at Kota Bharu, 13 500 men landed at Singora and 7550 at Patani — a total of 26 640 of whom 17 000 were combat troops. Yamashita himself, who had travelled in on a transport, was among the first wave to land at Singora.

On the Kota Bharu front, Brigadier B. W. Key who was commanding the 8th Indian Brigade, tried to rally his men, but it was a hopeless task. And Yamashita had effectively forestalled MATADOR for which the troops of the 11th Indian Division had been standing by at thirty minutes notice in drenching rain since the afternoon of the sixth.

When all his units were safely ashore, Yamashita could signal

Tokyo that he was beginning his long 650 km push down the tail of the peninsula that would end only when his XXV Army reached Singapore. Already he had given the city a taste of what was to come by sending down a wave of aircraft to attack the almost defenceless city which was now just seventy days away from its final humiliation.

Shell-Shock

At quarter past one on the morning of the landings at Kota Bharu, Monday 8 December 1941, the Governor and Commander-in-Chief of Singapore, Sir Shenton Thomas, was awakened by a telephone call from General Percival, the GOC Malaya. Percival, who was calling from military headquarters at Fort Canning, told Thomas that the Japanese had landed in three places near the Thai border. Shenton replied, 'I suppose you'll shove the little men off.' Then after waking his wife and the servants, he sent a message to his Colonial Secretary warning him to stand by.

He and his wife drank their coffee together on the wide first-floor balcony of Government House, looking down on the peaceful scene of the port and the city spread out before them. The city was brilliantly lit, as it always was, and he could see the silhouette of the Cathay Building, tallest on the island, and the whiteness of the government buildings. A bright moon lit up the still crowded harbour and if this was to be the start of the war, he reflected, it all looked and felt absurdly normal.

A little overweight and perhaps — or so his critics said — enjoying the trappings of office (the yacht that went with the job, the cockaded topee and the great palace of a house) rather too much, he was in no way a pompous man. And his severest critics never questioned that he cared very much about the people that he ruled. And ruled was not too strong a word.

There was no pretence that the Crown Colony of Singapore was a democracy. As Governor of the Straits Settlements, as his formal title described him (Singapore, Penang and Malacca were the three settlements), he was appointed by the British Colonial office and ruled by decree.

Thomas was also High Commissioner for the Malay States, a complicated political arrangement of once autonomous states which were now ruled indirectly by Britain whose primary concern was their tin and rubber. There were four Federated Malay States which had Sultans who still occupied their thrones although they were largely governed by a central administration in Kuala Lumpur; and six Unfederated States, which had resisted federation. These six were still directly ruled by their Sultans although they had a British adviser with an administrative staff that was almost exclusively British at the higher, decision-making levels.

Five of the Unfederated States were in Malaya and the sixth was Brunei, 1300 km away in Borneo. The most important of them, and always the best ruled, was Johore whose capital Johore Bahru lay at the northern end of the causeway on to Singapore. The Sultan of Johore, Sir Ibrahim, with whom General Gordon Bennett had struck up such friendly relations, was a shrewd ruler who in 1941 had been on the throne for 46 years.

British political control over the peninsula had transformed the country economically and socially. As the Romans had done in Britain, the British in Malaya gave much attention to transport. A railway ran from north to south and a broad road network, which was to prove so invaluable to the Japanese, was constructed. Many stretches of it were paved to withstand the tropical rains. Penang and Singapore and a number of smaller ports were enlarged and improved and all in all it was a very prosperous and orderly little country.

There were periodic clashes between the two main races, the Chinese and the Malays, who were very poorly integrated, but these made hardly a ripple on the overall calm of life in Malaya. The Europeans in the early forties before the Japanese landed accounted for only one half of one per cent of the 5.5 million population and the Chinese and Malays, in roughly equal numbers, (the Chinese slightly outnumbered the Malays) totalled nearly 85 per cent. The rest were principally Indians from southern India who worked as coolies on the plantations.

The Chinese were far more astute and adapted to a life in industry and commerce than the easy-going Malays, but they were relatively new arrivals. The first significant Chinese immigration had occurred less than thirty years earlier when they came looking for tin. Their success in almost every sphere of life on the peninsula created resentment among the Malays. The Japanese would later exploit this to the full.

There was, however an air of well-being over Malaya which was not seriously affected by the rumours of Japanese threats which were being increasingly voiced. The British had promised that the population would always be protected and there had never been a serious threat to their peace in the lives of any of them.

It was this promise, believed implicitly by people of every race, which made it all the more treacherous in the eyes of many when the British, after taking no steps to provide protection for Malaya by way of fixed defences, aircraft or strong garrisons, just walked out on the population and left them to their own devices and to the mercy of the Japanese.

Sir Shenton Thomas, for whom these nightmares were still in the future, spent the next two hours dressing and waiting impatiently for more news. At about quarter to four he walked out on to the lawn in front of the house, which was bathed in moonlight, and he was pacing up and down when he received another phone call. This time it was Air Vice-Marshal Pulford, the Air Force Chief, who told him urgently that Japanese aircraft were heading for the island and were within 40 km of the city. Pulford said that his Operations Room had endeavoured to contact the ARP to have the city's lights turned out, but that nobody had answered the phone.

Thomas barely had time to warn the Harbour Board when he heard the drone of aircraft overhead and almost simultaneously the crash of the first bombs falling. It was exactly 4.15.

The previous evening, Edward Koek, a lawyer and Member of the Legislative Council, and his wife Cynthia had spent a leisurely Sunday visiting friends and playing tennis On most Sundays a group of about fourteen of them played tennis or swam in the afternoon and then went back to one or other of their homes for dinner and to play cards.

Cynthia Koek was a cheerful and popular part of the social scene in Singapore, married to a man she adored, well off and blissfully unaware of the dangers that lay ahead. She had been a promising actress in London until a freak riding accident abruptly cut short her career. When she was twenty her horse bolted and carried her straight through a stable door, crushing her leg against the side. That same evening she had been due to appear in Diaghilev's Russian Ballet but instead she lay in hospital, her leg amputated.

51

Her fiancé, Edward Koek, had come straight to England from Singapore and as soon as she could walk, he married her and took her back to the island with him. She had been there now for twenty years and in the dark days that lay ahead, she would be taken into captivity by the Japanese, beaten, accused by her friends of collaboration and, because she had only one leg and could not go on work parties, given the filthiest job of cleaning the prison latrines.

Some time after dinner the Koeks and their friends drove down to the beach at Bedok, 15 km to the east of the city on the road to Changi. They sat on the wall looking out across the water, listening to it lapping under their feet. A big moon was rising, a harvest moon. When the Koeks got home to Tanglin at about half past twelve, it was such a lovely night that Edward suggested they sit for a while in the garden. And that was where the two of them were when suddenly the night was shattered by an enormous crash and the sky seemed to be filled with the noise of aircraft.

In fact it was not as severe a raid as the Japanese had planned. When the ground troops were well ashore at Kota Bharu, the aircraft had been despatched from an airfield in Indo-China. The raid was intended to serve a dual purpose: to give due warning to the population of Singapore that the Japanese were on their way south, and to neutralise the airfields from which they expected Allied aircraft to take off to attack their landing forces.

The damage they caused would have been greater than it was if they had not run into foul weather on the way down to Singapore which kept the bombers at wave-top height and forced half of them to return to base. Seventeen flew on towards Singapore. By about 4.00 a.m. when they were approaching the island, the weather had cleared and the moon was lighting up the harbour and the city.

Not that the pilots needed the moon to guide them in because from miles away they could see Singapore with all its lights burning as usual and all their targets brilliantly illuminated.

The Japanese concentrated their attack on the Seletar and Tengah airfields to the west and north of the city, but did little damage to them. A few bombs fell on the waterfront and the city centre, one in Raffles Place the main square of the city, but these were probably all intended for the Kallang Airfield that was almost in the middle of the town.

The greatest casualties were suffered when a bomb fell in

Chinatown. Inevitably in the cramped, over-crowded conditions there, it caused much damage. In all, sixty civilians were killed and twice that number wounded, and a few buildings were damaged.

Many people watched the raids from windows or suburban gardens and thought that it was a realistic practice by British aircraft. Some of the Japanese pilots dived to release their bombs, while others made low-level runs. The anti-aircraft guns fired noisily but ineffectually and a few men fired their rifles hopefully in the general direction of the planes. None of the aircraft were seriously damaged.

Three Australian Buffalos had been alerted and warmed up, but in fact no Allied fighters were sent up to try and drive off the raiders in spite of the fact that the bombers presented a perfect target. Afterwards Pulford explained that he was so concerned at the incompetence of the anti-aircraft gunners and by the real likelihood that they would shoot down his own aircraft instead of the Japanese, that he refused to allow them to take off.

Radar had detected the Japanese more than half an hour before they arrived, but the Operations Room had not been able to get a reply from the civil ARP headquarters. By the time Pulford rang the Governor, there was not enough time for him to take any steps.

The defence chiefs could have given the order to black out the city, as far as that was possible in a short time, but since one o'clock they had all been closeted in conference discussing the implications of the landing at Kota Bharu and on the Kra Isthmus. Apparently nobody thought that there was a risk of a raid on the island.

When the Japanese attacked Pearl Harbour at 7.55 in the morning Hawaiian time, their attack was again such a surprise that the aircraft were not even recognised as being hostile until the bombs started falling.

An hour after the Japanese had gone, someone turned off the city's lights. Next morning, if the population had reason to be grateful that the casualties were not more serious, they were severely shaken by the events of the previous night.

Why had Singapore's lights not been turned off, they asked. And when it was known soon after 1.00 a.m. that the Japanese had landed in Malaya, why were Japanese aircraft allowed to get to within 40 km of the city before anyone even knew they were there? And why were alarms not sounded so that people could take cover?

For the first time people questioned their unswerving belief that they lived in an impregnable fortress.

By breakfast the news had also been broken of the raid on Pearl Harbour. But ironically the entry of the Americans into the war which immediately followed the attack, only reinforced the belief of the population in Singapore that they were in some way exempt from danger.

The morning saw too the release of the first of a string of downright silly and misleading communiqués issued by GHQ. Hard on the revelation that the Japanese had landed in three places to their north, that the US Navy had been decimated, that Singapore had been bombed with impunity, came an Order of the Day signed by Brooke-Popham as Commander-in-Chief, Far East, praising Allied preparedness and strength and belittling the weakness of a Japan 'drained for years by the exhausting claims of her wanton onslaught on China'.

If it was intended to raise the morale of the Indian soldiers in Malaya, as Brooke-Popham later maintained, it had exactly the opposite effect on the civilians in Singapore. They wondered what the strong Japanese would do to them if the exhausted ones could attack their city with such impunity. And the Indians themselves knew much better than GHQ what it was like to face the Japanese.

Brooke-Popham said later that he had written the report some time before the raid to allow it to be translated into all the languages spoken in the Far East. But he did not explain why nobody had stopped its distribution some eight hours after the attack.

The London *Daily Mail* remarked in a leader after it had heard of the incident, 'Events in the Far East would have been less of a shock if Air Chief-Marshal Sir Robert Brooke-Popham had stuck to strategy and avoided oratory.'

The first War Communiqué issued from GHQ in Singapore was equally false, the first in a long series of lies and half-truths that achieved nothing except add to the complacency. The communiqué said that the Japanese had been répulsed at Kota Bharu and that only a few bombs had fallen and these harmlessly on an airfield outside the town. 'All surface craft are retiring at high speed,' it said, referring to the Japanese, 'and the few troops left on the beach have been heavily machine-gunned.'

The initial shock of the raid had a curious effect on the European population. Instead of depression and worry that their impregnable fortress might, after all, be built on sand, there was an almost exaggerated air of heartiness and bonhomie as though people were playing some kind of bizarre game and pretending that the raid had never happened and that the Japanese did not exist.

There was a rush to buy black-out material from Robinsons, the department store, but apart from that life went on exactly as normal. There were no more raids on the Monday or all day on Tuesday and on Tuesday evening there was the usual dinner dance at Raffles to the music of Don Hopkins's Orchestra playing old-fashioned dance music. It wasn't quite as usual because the hotel had not been able to finish blacking-out the windows so that the dance had to be held in near-darkness.

The evening ended abruptly with the wailing of the air raid siren. Waiters fled and the dancers made their way home, but it was a false alarm. In fact there were no more raids on the city for nearly three weeks although other targets on the island, mainly the airfields and ammunition and fuel dumps, were attacked every few days.

If there was widespread relief that the bombing had not been repeated, the relaxation lulled the population back into its old apathy. People were even saying bravely that the Japanese now realised that Singapore was too well defended and too risky a target to try bombing it again.

Up in the north of the peninsula, meanwhile, nobody had any such illusions and the havoc being wrought by the Japanese landings was being made worse by an almost total breakdown in Allied communications. In the darkness and rain the troops who had not already fled before the Japanese were withdrawn from their forward positions if they could be contacted. Some units could not be reached and were lost altogether.

Others had to cross a flooded river over which the bridge that they had hoped to use had collapsed and some were swept away while others were left behind to be massacred or captured by the Japanese.

The Japanese had complete air mastery over Kota Bharu and their air offensive was so successful that within 48 hours of the landing, the equivalent of three bomber squadrons and one fighter squadron had been lost in the air and on the ground. The remaining aircraft that could get away limped back towards the south.

As the Allies were forced to abandon one aerodrome after another because the defending forces at each one were so small in numbers and so weak in resolve that they collapsed almost as soon as the Japanese came in sight, an attempt was made to put a scorched earth policy into effect. But the sound of the explosions and the great columns of smoke that marked the burning fuel, had such a demoralising effect on the Indian troops that orders had to be given that in future petrol and oil were to be allowed to run to waste and not set alight.

The monsoon which the Allies had expected to hinder and prevent Japanese landings had in fact made their approach much easier and more effective by providing them with cloud cover. Yamashita's insistence that he be allowed to begin the attack on Malaya when he did and not wait until Japan had mastery of the high seas, had been amply vindicated. And now the rains had so affected the roads along which reinforcements should have been moved by the defenders, that counter-attack was all but impossible.

Percival was in a dilemma. He knew which Indian units would fight bravely to the end — invariably the ones with good British officers at their head and with a British unit fighting alongside them — and he knew what a minority these were. If he ordered the Indian troops to stand and fight to the death, therefore, the field would either be quickly littered with their bodies, or more likely the order would be disobeyed. Neither result would do anything to help his cause.

But the Japanese were not even being inconvenienced by the opposition that he could put up against them. He had considered sending up the 8th Australian Division to relieve the 11th Indian Division which was in tatters, but from London Churchill cautioned him against losing too many troops too soon or having them cut off on the Peninsula. Churchill's admonition that 'nothing compares in importance with the Fortress' caused him to change his mind.

If he were to limit his losses on the ground, the only feasible way was to order limited withdrawals whenever a unit was threatened with being cut off and this was the course that he decided to follow.

In Singapore, the service chiefs followed with a sense of increasing gloom the reports coming back from the front. They knew now that while Malaya was being attacked, the great naval and air base at Pearl Harbour on Oahu Island, Hawaii had been attacked at 7.55 a.m. on 7 December* destroying or damaging 19 ships, including 4 battleships sunk and 1 run aground, and 120 planes. Casualties totalled 2403 dead and 1178 wounded.

It had soon become clear that even this was not the limit of the Japanese offensive. As well as Pearl Harbour, Thailand and Malaya, they had launched attacks at Midway, Guam and Wake Islands (all key stages in the lifeline between the United States and the Philippines) on the Philippines themselves, on Ocean Island and on Hong Kong which was defended by two British, two Canadian and two Indian battalions.

Hong Kong was even more abandoned than Singapore. The British and Indian battalions had lost many of their most experienced officers and men to places which were thought more worth defending. The artillery on the island dated from World War I and had to be hauled around by Chinese-owned trucks whose drivers bartered with the Army whenever the guns needed to be moved. But the casualties were no joke — 11 848 combatants lost in the fighting, and unimaginable brutality by the Japanese after the surrender.

In Singapore no one fumed more than Admiral Sir Tom Phillips but he at least had the means of making a contribution to the fighting that was going on in the north. On 2 December, the battleship HMS *Prince of Wales* and the battle cruiser HMS *Repulse* had arrived in Singapore and were tied up in the naval base, their crews restless to go into battle.

In August and September the question of sending a battle fleet to Singapore had been under daily discussion in London. The importance of the Navy in any successful defence of Singapore was clear enough to the Admiralty, but since the fall of France there had just not been suitable ships to send.

As a partial answer, the Admiralty had recommended that four World War I battleships should be sent to the Indian Ocean and reinforced early in 1942 with two more slow battleships, a battle cruiser and in an emergency an aircraft carrier.

Churchill, however, opposed this plan and wanted to send the

---

*Because Hawaii was on the other side of the International Date Line, the day was a day earlier than in Malaya.

newly completed battleship *Duke of York* together with an old but fast battle cruiser and an aircraft carrier which, he said, would all have a paralysing effect on neighbourhood action.

The Admiralty replied that neither the *Duke of York* nor the other two battleships which had recently joined the fleet could be spared as long as there was any possibility of the new German battleship *Tirpitz* moving into the Atlantic. They added that in their belief any British fleet which was smaller than the fleet which Japan was likely to employ (the Japanese had ten battleships at the time) was unlikely to be a deterrent that would keep them out of the Indian Ocean. The argument continued but Churchill had his way and late in October, the Admiralty agreed to send the *Prince of Wales* and the *Repulse*, together with the aircraft carrier *Indomitable*, to Singapore.

Before they could leave, however, *Indomitable* ran aground in Jamaica during a training cruise and no other carrier could be spared. When it was realised that no carrier could accompany the other two ships to give them air defence, the whole exercise should have been abandoned.

Even before *Indomitable* went aground, the First Lord and the First Sea Lord strongly opposed the whole exercise, and Jan Smuts, the South African leader, telegraphed a prophetic warning of the dangers that were likely to ensue if the ships were allowed to go. But again Churchill was adamant.

The ships received a tumultuous welcome when they arrived in Singapore. The overwhelming feeling of relief, almost of elation, almost seemed to justify the enormous risk that Churchill was taking. Not only in Singapore itself, but throughout Malaya, it was interpreted as meaning that the British had made good their promise and were coming to the aid of the Fortress. People said confidently that now the Japanese would have to pull their necks in.

Duff Cooper had been at the naval base to greet them and like everyone else that day had been thrilled by the sight of the ships, with their four destroyer escorts, sailing round the bend into the narrow straits. As nothing else had done, they conferred a sense of complete — and completely false — security on almost everyone who saw them. The lack of an aircraft carrier did not have the same significance to the people of Singapore as it did to the senior service officers who were appalled at the way that Churchill could risk so many lives for what they saw as nothing more than a political gimmick.

Nor did anybody seem to notice that apart from the *Prince of Wales* and the *Repulse*, the only ships based in Singapore were three small, outdated cruisers, seven destroyers of which four were small and obsolete, three gun boats and an assortment of smaller craft that included six tugs and various motor launches. A cruiser and three destroyers in addition to these were in Singapore, including the Australian ships HMAS *Vampire* and *Vendetta*, but they belonged to other stations and were only there for refits.

To Phillips it seemed unthinkable that a powerful naval force should be sitting uselessly in harbour while Allied land and air forces were being pulverised by the Japanese a few hundred kilometres to the north. If for no other reason he believed that he had to act to prevent the public asking what on earth the ships were doing in Singapore at all if they were not allowed to fight.

It must have been the hardest decision of his life to take those ships out knowing that if luck deserted him, his venture could only end in tragedy.

With no air cover from a supporting carrier, he asked Air Vice-Marshal Pulford to give him protection from land air-bases, but he received only a non-committal reply. None the less, he decided that he would proceed with his plan to attack the Japanese invasion force at dawn on 10 December. He thought it almost certain that when it came to the battle, Pulford would give him the air cover he needed.

Code-named 'Z' Force, the *Prince of Wales* and the *Repulse*, with an escort of four destroyers that included the *Vampire*, sailed from the base at 5.35 p.m. on the evening of 8 December. It was a very subdued departure compared with the tumultuous welcome that they had received a week earlier.

Phillips sailed up the coast, 'looking for trouble', as he told the flagship's company. He would find it soon enough. He steered a course that took him east of the Anambas Islands to avoid possible enemy mines near the coast, and he had been at sea for only a short time when a signal came that there would be no air support. Indeed, he never had any justification for assuming that he would receive it.

By mid-afternoon on 10 December the battleship and the cruiser lay at the bottom of the sea, unable to defend themselves against

Japanese torpedo bombers. Admiral Phillips and the *Prince of Wales's* captain, Captain J. C. Leach, went down with their ship, while 845 highly trained naval personnel were lost. For the Admiralty, who had always had the gravest misgivings about sending the two capital ships in the first place, it was a chilling vindication of the stand they had taken to try to dissuade Churchill.

Churchill learned the news while he was opening his dispatch boxes in bed before getting up, as was his custom. 'In all the war,' he wrote later, 'I never received a more direct shock. As I turned over and twisted in bed, the full horror of the news sank in upon me. There were no British or American capital ships in the Indian Ocean or the Pacific except the American survivors of Pearl Harbour. Over all this vast expanse of waters, Japan was supreme and we everywhere were weak and naked.' So far as the *Prince of Wales* and *Repulse* were concerned, he and the families and friends of the 845 men who lay at the bottom of the South China Sea, had no one to blame but himself.

In the whole terrible, inexcusable tragedy, the only redeeming feature was the extraordinary bravery of the men on the two ships and the destroyer crews who sailed in through the fire and the bombs to drag survivors clear. Had it not been for their gallantry, the death toll would have been far higher. The men on the doomed ships also behaved with superb coolness and courage. 'Here,' said an RAF pilot who flew over the scene for an hour, 'was something above human nature.'

The news was received in Singapore by servicemen and civilians alike with stunned disbelief. Duff Cooper said, 'That was the worst single piece of news I have ever received. More disastrous things, such as the fall of France have happened, but the news of them arrived gradually and the mind had time to prepare itself for the catastrophe.' It was left to Duff Cooper to broadcast the news of the disaster to the people of Singapore that night.

As the defenders on the land were pushed back the Allied Air Force fell back too. Soon it had only 50 aircraft left fit for operations. Most of these were withdrawn and limped back to Singapore. Against them the Japanese now had 530 aeroplanes in the battle zone and continued to demonstrate that they were neither night-blind nor myopic, but excellent airmen with superior machines. Dutch air reinforcements sent in from Java had to be hurriedly withdrawn when it was realised that the pilots had not been trained to fly at night.

On land, the Japanese troops were forging their way inland and fanning out across the peninsula. They encountered little serious opposition and the information provided by their intelligence units had told them precisely where to expect resistance.

As they hurried southwards, with many of them on bicycles, they sometimes looked so similar to the Malays that the defending forces thought they were friendly. The Japanese showed that they could move so silently that they were in amongst the Allied troops before they even knew what was happening to them. As Bennett had so accurately predicted, few things had a more demoralising effect on the Indians than the sudden appearance in their midst of wildly screaming Japanese soldiers charging straight at them from every direction with fixed bayonets.

For the Japanese, trained in jungle warfare, the terrain, as Bennett had again predicted, was friendly and provided them with cover and the element for surprise. For the Indians and, with only a few conspicuous exceptions, the British units attached to the Indian Corps, it was a dripping, hateful, hostile environment in which they were completely out of place.

Without a single tank in Malaya, the Allies found themselves up against Japanese tanks in country where Percival and his advisers had said that tanks could never operate.

By 13 December the island and important base of Penang, off the Malayan west coast, was being heavily bombarded and was in imminent danger of being over-run. In spite of a promise by the Allies to the people of Penang that the Europeans would never desert them, but would stay with them to the end if they were threatened by the Japanese, the order was given for the immediate evacuation of all European women, children and hospital patients.

Already there were ghastly stories circulating of what the Japanese had done to the innocent civilians in other towns they had captured and the decision to evacuate the place was the only one that the administration could have responsibly taken. But many of the Europeans who were made to leave in this way, did so very reluctantly and with the belief that they were betraying a people who had always shown them loyalty.

Two days later their shame increased further when the War Council that had been formed ordered a total evacuation of the garrison and any remaining Europeans. By now Penang was not only undefendable, but it was in grave danger of falling victim to a major outbreak of cholera or typhoid. There were unburied bodies everywhere and broken sanitary facilities spilled their contents into gardens and over the roads.

Those Malays who wanted to leave joined the long and sorry procession of refugees who streamed south down the peninsula ahead of the Japanese, heading for what they believed was the sanctuary of the Fortress on Singapore. Many more remained behind to protect other members of their families who refused to flee.

The island fell shortly afterwards and the Japanese encountered no resistance at all. Many of the supplies on the base were destroyed before the defending garrison left, but the powerful radio transmitter and broadcasting station were left intact and were soon being used by the Japanese to broadcast propaganda all over South-East Asia. Many small boats too were left undamaged on the harbour and were put to use by the Japanese.

Less than a month later, on 11 January, Kuala Lumpur the capital of the Federated Malay States, was abandoned by the British in the same way and fell to the Japanese without opposition.

A great convoy had started to roll southwards out of the city on the previous day, a Saturday, with a strange array of vehicles, from Rolls Royces to fire engines, all requisitioned by the military. The official historian wrote, 'The white *tuans* had indeed been humbled. Not only were they giving up great military, commercial and personal possessions; they were being forced to leave behind them millions of Asians whom they were pledged to protect.'

The Japanese entered Kuala Lumpur at eight o'clock in the evening on Sunday the 11th and unlike Penang, found that civil authority had completely broken down with the departure of the Europeans. Their immediate priority was to disperse huge mobs of looters who were roaming through the city, stealing and breaking what they chose. After a few very public executions they quickly put an end to that problem, as they would do a few weeks later in Singapore in an even more gruesome manner.

Almost more than in Penang, the Japanese had reason to be grateful for what the retreating Europeans had left for them. Huge quantities of stores waited undestroyed and undamaged in the warehouses. Even the airfield was serviceable and could be used immediately for extending the air attacks on Singapore.

By the middle of December, Percival knew that the most he could hope for was to slow the Japanese down in the hope that every extra day would give the reinforcements a greater chance of arriving in time. He took heart from the fact that when the Japanese reached Johore, they would at least come up against Bennett and the AIF who would put up a much stiffer resistance than the Indians had done.

Percival's plan called for the establishment of a strong line of defence about 200 km from Singapore running roughly from Mersing in the east, through Segamat on the main trunk road, to Muar in the west. The western half of this line was to be defended by III Indian Corps, while the east would be held by the two AIF brigades.

Bennett's men were already in their defensive positions extending from the east coast across to the trunk road. The weather was appalling. The Australians were suffering badly in the monsoon from endless mosquito bites that were driving them mad and infecting them with malaria, and from the tropical sores that ate into their legs.

Typical of the discomfort they endured was that recorded by Frank Hole, a private with 2/20th Battalion. Hole and his mate spent night after night trying to sleep in the mud, with their groundsheet wrapped round their bren gun to keep it dry; and as they slept, the ground became softer and softer and they sank deeper into the mud until almost no part of them could be seen above the ground.

The weather stayed like that until about Christmas and even the food had to be floated across swollen rivers on table tops by men who took it in turn to swim over to the ration truck waiting on the other side.

By Christmas too Percival was becoming increasingly irritated by Bennett who persisted in asking the Australian government, through his own channel of communication, for reinforcements. Percival wanted replacements as much as Bennett, but he objected to Bennett behaving as though he was the Commander-in-Chief of a separate Australian army which just happened to be fighting alongside his own.

Bennett had already established his right to have direct access to his minister and there was nothing that Percival could do about that. On 27 December he tried another tack and gave orders that in future nobody under his command was to apply direct to a Dominion government for additional manpower or equipment.

He presumably expected Bennett to object — although he had deliberately not named Bennett in his order — but what he did not anticipate was that the Australian would simply refuse to obey him. Bennett told him bluntly that he had a responsibility above all else to his government in Australia, and that on any matter which affected the security of the AIF he would continue to communicate directly with them. Percival's protests to his Chiefs of Staff were in vain, not one imagines because their sympathies lay with Bennett, but because they had more than enough on their hands without inviting a political skirmish with the Australian government.

Bennett never refused to obey a tactical order given to him by Percival, but he was not at all happy with the way the British general was using the forces at his disposal. In particular, he believed that the weakly defended western side of the peninsula, where Percival had positioned a small force of the Indians, almost as a reserve, was much more vulnerable than the east. The Japanese could land there without opposition, he argued, and cut off the Australian retreat back to the island. A west coast landing would also give the Japanese a good second route into Singapore along the coast road.

Bennett also believed, probably correctly, that the Australians offered the only remaining chance for the Allies to stop the Japanese in their headlong rush towards Singapore; and that even if this were only a temporary respite, the extra few days might make the difference between the reinforcements arriving in time or too late. It did not occur to anyone that the reinforcements might not be coming at all.

Bennett wanted to have control of the trunk road down the centre which he was sure Yamashita would use for his main force, as well as the western sector. The good road surface would allow him to speed up his tanks and other mobile forces in an effort to outflank the Australians defending Johore.

Bennett made no secret of his belief that many of the withdrawals that had taken place had been the result of bad leadership as much as bad troops. He was determined to show how his Australians would behave in battle. As the remnants of III Indian Corps limped back towards Johore to take up their position at the western end of the line, he proposed to Percival that when the last of them had safely withdrawn, all the forces in Johore should come under his command including the British and Indians.

Alternatively he wanted the AIF to be switched from the east coast to the west where he saw the greatest danger.

Percival, however, also had enough problems of his own without inviting the reaction that he knew would follow from everybody else if Bennett was given overall command. And he still believed that the greatest threat lay in the east and that he would be weakening his defences there too much if the 22nd Australian Brigade was shifted over to the west as Bennett suggested. The only troops who would be available to replace the Australians were men of III Indian Corps and that to all intents and purposes, as Bennett himself knew full well, meant that the east would be virtually undefended. He therefore denied Bennett both his requests.

On the grounds that this decision jeopardised the safety of Australian forces, Bennett predictably and immediately went over Percival's head and complained to the Australian government, adding that Heath's III Corps was 'tired and lacking in determination'.

The problem was resolved towards the end of the first week in 1942 when General Sir Archibald Wavell, the new Supreme Commander of the combined American, British, Dutch and Australian troops (ABDA) in the Far East, visited Malaya on his way to Java. It was his first visit in his new official capacity and by ill coincidence — though not for Bennett — he arrived just as Heath's Indian troops were taking their most crushing defeat at Slim River, 160 km further north.

For the 11th Indian Infantry Division Slim River was a death blow and from that day it ceased to exist as a fighting unit. The battle also gave a new impetus to Bennett's proposal and after Wavell had inspected the survivors among the Indian troops, he ordered that the Australians were to be given the centre of the peninsula to defend including the main trunk road as Bennett had requested. He also put Bennett in command of operations in the west.

Bennett's 22nd Brigade, however, was to remain in the east and was put under the command of General Heath's III Corps.

Wavell seems to have been as impressed by Bennett as the Australian was with him and in his report he said that he was confident that Bennett would put up 'a very active defense'. The Australians wanted nothing more than to be given the opportunity of doing just that.

Retreat

On the way up through Singapore, Wavell had made another discovery which disturbed him even more than the disastrous defeat at Slim River. In complete disbelief, as he said afterwards, he saw that the much vaunted defences that he, like everyone else, had always assumed would protect the island against any land-based attack, did not exist. 'No defences had been made or even planned in detail on the north side of the island,' he wrote, 'although it was obvious by now that we might be driven back into the island and have to defend it.'

There was not one fortification or one gun position to cope with the eventuality. All those years of British propaganda had succeeded beyond anyone's dreams — it had been so successful that even the British generals had fallen headlong into the trap of believing it themselves.

The Japanese had been firmly ashore on Malayan soil on 8 December. There was no doubt from that moment that their final destination was Singapore. But incredibly it was not until 23 December that Percival took any steps to arrange for defence positions to be prepared in the north. Even then all that he did was to order the Commander of the Singapore Fortress, Major-General Keith Simmons to 'arrange for a reconnaissance of the north shore of Singapore Island to select positions for the defence of possible landing places'.

Simmons apparently gave the job low priority and released only a few officers for the job so that by the time Wavell came through, almost nothing had still been done.

After nearly forty years it is still impossible to understand how it happened. Percival was after all the acknowledged authority on the defence of Singapore and owed his present position as GOC to this expertise.

If an attack had come from the sea — which Percival had been the first to point out was unlikely — Singapore would certainly have been able to put up a very strong defence. And one of the misconceptions that has persisted is that the big guns were on a fixed line of fire pointing out to sea and could not be turned against the Japanese if they came down from the north. In fact all the big 15-inch guns could traverse through 360° and three 9.2-inch guns of Connaught Battery, sited on Sentosa Island near the city, as well as the two 6-inch guns all had arcs of fire that included the northern approaches from the mainland.

It was not the direction of these guns that was the problem, but their ammunition. As they had been intended for firing at ships, their basic ammunition was armour-piercing, deadly against warships, but almost entirely ineffective against personnel, artillery or land targets because the heavy shells buried themselves in the soft ground before they detonated.

What was needed for knocking out most ground targets was high-explosive shells and of these there were very few for the larger weapons. The 15-inch guns had none at all while the 9.2-inch guns had only about thirty rounds apiece. As they were supposed to be holding out for six months, they could afford to fire about one round a week.

A second drawback of using the big guns against land targets was that they fired in a relatively flat trajectory — ideal for shooting out to sea at ships, but of little use against an enemy who was dug in. The shells just went over their heads.

The guns also had no overhead protection against an attack from the air because it had been assumed that they would rely for their defence on fighter aircraft, of which there were now very few, and on anti-aircraft guns. However most of these on the island were medium-range weapons and were unable to hit the bombers which flew over the island just out of range.

By the time the Japanese reached the Straits of Johore, the Allies would not even have any observation posts on the mainland which were the only means of warning the anti-aircraft gunners that enemy planes were approaching. They were therefore never prepared.

For the same reason the occupation of Johore by the Japanese would mean that for much of the time the fixed defence guns on the island would be firing blind. Because of the jungle and the terrain on Johore and the relative flatness of Singapore, the Japanese would always be hidden from the view of the gunners and aerial spotting would be impossible because the Japanese had control of the air.

There had been elaborate plans in existence for years for fortifying Johore, but they had lain in a desk in Whitehall, postponed and ignored. The problem was largely one of money because fixed defences across the whole peninsula, which were recommended, would be extremely expensive. There was then the additional problem that any effective defence would have to include strong air power to protect those defences once they were built. And once there was strong air power, it would need still more aircraft to defend the air-fields from which they would operate.

These aircraft had never been available and there was every indication that they never would, but the notion had persisted that in a crisis the naval base would always be protected from the mainland and this became one more reason for putting the island's own fixed defences out of mind.

Like all the other fixed defences that did exist on Singapore, the beach defences were in the wrong place and had been designed to meet attack from the sea. Almost all the thinking on the island's defence had been formulated in the time when aeroplanes were not able to fly far enough to pose a serious threat to Singapore from anywhere to the north.

The fixed defences included concrete machine-gun pill boxes every 500 m, 18-pounder field guns and anti-tank and anti-boat obstacles, searchlights and barbed wire. There were also land-mines, but the climate was so humid that many of them had corroded and become useless and they were all so dangerous that there was no way of establishing which of them if any were still live.

Behind these beach defences were two 'switch' lines which would play a part in the battle that would soon be raging across the island. They were lines on the map behind which the defenders could take up a position to resist a successful landing on either the east or west coasts.

In the east the Serangoon Line covered Kallang Airfield and ran north to the Serangoon River; and on the west, the Jurong Line stretched across the five kilometre neck of land between the head of the Kranji River which flowed north into the Johore Strait and the Jurong River which ran south into the sea.

There had been plans for fortifying these two switch lines for years, but nothing had been done. Even though work was started to dig an anti-tank ditch along the Jurong Line after Wavell's visit, it proved to be no deterrent at all when it was put to the test.

Writing after the war, Percival said that he had always intended to start the actual construction of the defences at the beginning of January and that he was about to begin when Wavell arrived. But Brigadier I. Simson, the Chief Engineer of Malayan Command, maintained that this was not true.

On the contrary, said Simson, who was recognised as a very able engineer, it was he who was strongly urging Percival to allow him to begin building defensive positions to cover Johore Strait and that Percival refused and was still refusing when Wavell came.

After the war Simson related an extraordinary conversation that he said occurred when he went to see Percival at this time just as the general was about to go to bed. Unshaven and dishevelled because he had come straight from work after midnight, Simson felt obliged to raise yet again his grave concern about the lack of any defences in the north. He had sought permission many times to at least make a start but Percival always refused yet gave no reason that made any sense to Simson.

On this night he made an eloquent plea to start work immediately so that, as he put it, 'The water surface of the strait and the shore line would be the main killing areas.' He explained that he would like fixed and semi-permanent defences, anti-tank defences, mines, anchored and floating barbed wire and fire.

Percival heard him out and then as usual turned his request down flat; but this time Simson demanded an explanation for Percival's insistence on leaving nearly a million people exposed to the fast-approaching Japanese. Percival gave him his explanation. 'I believe defences like those you are suggesting,' he said baldly, 'would be bad for the morale of the troops and civilians.'

Simson said something about the effect on morale the arrival of the Japanese was likely to have and stormed out. It was 2.00 a.m. on the morning of 27 December, nineteen days after the landing at Kota Bharu.

If Simson was telling the truth — and there were other occasions when Percival's account of events as he described them several

69

years later, differed sharply from other people's recollections at the time — then one can only assume that either Percival believed that the Japanese would never reach the Johore Strait which seems inconceivable in view of the way the battle was going; or he concluded that if they did, they would still over-run the island no matter what defences he built. They would therefore be a waste of time and, as he confided in Simson, would achieve nothing but a lowering of morale. Again such defeatist thinking by the general charged with the defence of the island seems extraordinary.

Whatever the explanation, Percival must bear on his own shoulders a large share of the blame for what was to happen on Singapore. It is impossible to look at his failure to defend the island to the best of his ability, however limited that ability might have been, without remembering Yamashita's assertion that had the battle on Singapore lasted for even a few more days, the Japanese would almost certainly have been unable to hold out.

Wavell reported back to the Chiefs of Staff and to Churchill in London that the fate of Singapore now depended only on whether reinforcements arrived in time. When the Prime Minister read his report that 'little or nothing' had been done to build defences on the north of the island and that the guns would be almost useless, he was incredulous. 'The possibility of Singapore having no landward defences,' he lamented, 'no more entered my mind than that of a battleship being launched without a bottom.'

None of Churchill's immediate military advisers had mentioned this possibility and certainly Wavell himself had been unaware of the position until he saw it with his own eyes. But now, out of the blue, Churchill heard from the Director of Military Operations, Major-General Sir John Kennedy, that Singapore Island 'has never been considered defensible against close attack'. And he accurately went on to describe all the features which made that so, not least that Singapore was so small and flat and so near the mainland that all the vital installations would be within artillery range of the Japanese on Johore. It was for this reason, said Kennedy, that the Chiefs of Staff had always believed that a last-ditch defence of Singapore would have to take place in Johore rather than on the island.

Even this explanation though, would not have justified Percival's failure to take precautions because even by Kennedy's assessment, the role of the Fortress was to hold out for as long as possible until reinforcements arrived. That was what was meant by its impregnability.

Churchill however was not even convinced that Singapore would probably not hold out if Johore was lost. He sent off a volley of signals to his Chiefs and to Wavell telling him to use 'the entire male population under the most rigorous compulsion' to protect the island. Every piece of the island and especially the city of Singapore was to be 'defended to the death with no thought of surrender', or at the very least not until after protracted fighting 'among the ruins of the city'. Landing points were to be mined; barbed wire and booby traps placed in the swamps and artillery positioned to destroy the Japanese as they came across the strait.

Whatever the power of Churchill's oratory, Wavell was appalled by his order to defend Singapore to the death, seemingly regardless of the fate of the million helpless civilians. Mercifully for them Churchill's orders were disregarded.

Churchill, who until then had dismissed every plea for reinforcements, now at last took the situation seriously. He had always believed what his generals had told him, that Singapore was impregnable. Now they said that what they meant was that it was impregnable providing the mainland was defended. Singapore, the bastion of British supremacy in the Far East, was little more than an off-shore island with a few guns pointing out to sea.

He immediately arranged for Indian reinforcements who were waiting to sail to Burma to be diverted to Singapore. In a complete about-face, he invited the Australian government to consider moving I Australian Corps from Palestine to Singapore.

Whether these battle-hardened troops would have made any long-term difference to the campaign if they had been thrown into the fight is very doubtful, but Percival was never to find out. The Australian government's representative in Singapore, V. G. Bowden, cabled Cabinet that it should think very seriously before committing any further Australian troops to the Malayan campaign until guarantees had been received that the ones who were already there were not going to be abandoned.

Bowden's message happened to arrive just as War Cabinet's discussions were centred on the defence of Australia. It had already reached the conclusion that it needed the 7th Division back in Australia to protect its own country. Bowden's cable confirmed that this was the right decision.

Wavell gave orders to Percival that as a matter of the utmost priority defences must be built on the north coast. He told him to do it in complete secrecy to avoid alarm among the civilians, but at almost the same time Percival received other instructions from the Chiefs of Staff in London to prepare for the destruction of everything of military value on Singapore Island including the naval dockyard. Nothing could be more calculated to destroy morale than such action, which could clearly not be carried out in secret.

On 20 January Wavell returned to Singapore intending to inspect the new defences that Percival should by then have erected along the north and north-west coasts. To his anger he found that, despite his previous orders, in spite of the speed at which the Japanese were pushing down the peninsula and closing in on Singapore, Percival had still done nothing. The north coast was as naked and undefended as it had been before Wavell arrived on his first visit. He was furious.

The arrival of Wavell as Supreme Commander of ABDA meant that Duff Cooper was now without a job. For a month after the Japanese went to war and before Wavell arrived, he had presided over the hastily convened War Council which made immediate decisions affecting the war without any red tape or unnecessary paper work. It made proclamations on martial law, evacuation and the scorched earth policy, for example, while a sub-committee dealt with civil defence.

Wherever possible he tried to appoint one man to do a job rather than a committee, and so refreshing and effective was this that even after Wavell took up his appointment, there were many who wanted the minister to stay, including Wavell himself. He wanted to cable Churchill and ask him to leave Duff Cooper on the island because of his value.

It was Duff Cooper himself, however, who persuaded Wavell not to send it. He argued that he now had no position and therefore no authority. The conduct of the war was out of his hands, Brigadier Simson was organising civil defence and he was no longer even Resident Cabinet Minister. Wavell reluctantly conceded that he was right.

The *Straits Times* expressed the concern of many people outside the government when it said ruefully after the announcement that Duff Cooper was leaving: 'Singapore cannot, must not, be forced back to dependence on a system which has failed so dismally. Mr Duff Cooper is a man who can save us from that...' If Duff Cooper could not stay, the paper maintained, then Singapore should be given a Military Governor who could cut through the stupefying red tape that seemed to be inseparable from normal civilian government in the colony.

Duff Cooper didn't stay. As the Governor, Sir Shenton Thomas, took his place on the War Council, one imagines with a sense of considerable relief, Duff Cooper and his wife left Singapore just as a bombardment was falling on the airfield. Before they left their house for the last time, Diana Cooper said to a servant, 'Mix me a last gin sling.' The servant thought she said a large one and she arrived at the airport, as she said later, feeling well able to cope with the flight, the bombs and anything else the Japanese chose to throw at her.

They were hustled by some Chinese friends into an air-raid shelter made entirely from glass. 'It seemed,' wrote Duff Cooper, 'a suitable end to our mission in Singapore.'

As the war came closer to Johore and Singapore, there was a new feeling of excitement in the Australian lines as if they could smell the battle ahead. After five weeks of fighting, nine-tenths of the country had fallen into Japanese hands and the Australians, jungle-trained and impatient, had still not fired a shot in anger.

Bennett busied himself putting his troops into their new positions; not relaxing his training whenever the opportunity arose. His area of responsibility covered roughly half the peninsula, from the main road down the centre across to the west coast. It included a river crossing at the fishing port of Muar on the coast road.

As well as his own 27th Brigade, he had under his command the 45th Indian Brigade Group which had just arrived in Malaya, but was almost untrained let alone experienced in battle; and the remnants of the exhausted troops of the 9th Indian Division of III Corps which was still falling back across the Johore border. The 22nd, over on the east coast, was now under the command of General Heath.

For weeks Bennett had been planning a major ambush on the Japanese when they came into his area, which he was convinced was the only effective way of fighting them. He worked on the details with Brigadier Maxwell of the 27th Brigade and with Lieutenant-Colonel F. G. Galleghan of the 2/30th Battalion which would carry out the ambush. By the second week in January he was ready to put it into effect.

On the night of Tuesday 13 January the last of III Corps, except for a missing convoy of trucks, passed through Bennett's front line with the Japanese in hot pursuit. The place he had selected for the ambush was a stretch of the main Kuala Lumpur-Singapore road about 12 km west of Gemas on the Johore border. It was strictly in General Heath's area, but it had been agreed that Bennett would take it over for the ambush.

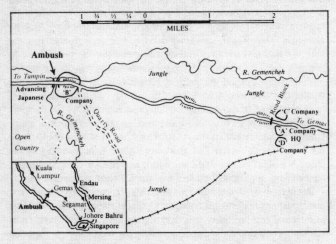

2/30th Battalion dispositions for Gemencheh ambush

The road crossed a wooden bridge over the small River Gemencheh at the position which Bennett had selected. On the Gemas side of this bridge there was a cutting, about four metres high, which ended only 60 m from the bridge, and this cutting together with the next 500 m of road was heavily jungled on both sides. It would be difficult or even impossible for the Japanese to escape.

On the Kuala Lumpur side of the bridge, the road ran straight for about 250 m and there was open ground on either side, so that here again the Japanese who were not caught in the first ambush would have nowhere to hide from the artillery and fighter fire that Bennett intended to call down.

Percival did not like the position on the grounds that it was too far ahead of the place where the main stand was to be made, about 12 km on the other side of Gemas, but Bennett insisted that it was ideal for an ambush.

Galleghan gave 'B' Company of his battalion the responsibility for manning the ambush itself while the other three companies and battalion headquarters went some 5 km further along the road towards Gemas. There they took up positions from north of the road to the railway line.

Near the bridge over the Gemencheh, a track known as Quarry Road ran towards the south. 'D' Company would withdraw along this when they had caused the greatest possible damage to the Japanese. To prevent those Japanese who were not caught in the ambush attempting a flanking movement round the Australians, two sections of the platoon, which was lying in wait in the cutting, were posted on each side of the road. From there they could cover both the road itself and the flats on either side of it.

In pouring rain they took up their positions. As Galleghan watched the minute hand of his watch ticking towards the deadline when the road would finally be closed, after which every vehicle and person would be treated as an enemy, his forward patrol warned that a convoy was approaching. They took cover and strained their eyes through the driving rain, waiting for their first glimpse of the Japanese. As the first vehicle rounded the corner, there was an almost audible release of tension as they saw that this was not the enemy, but the missing convoy of Indians racing for safety. Another five minutes and they would have been blasted off the road.

Another six hours passed and again word came from the forward patrols, this time that the Japanese really were approaching and travelling much faster than had been expected. Galleghan gave his orders. On either side of the road near the bridge, fingers tightened on triggers and the pins on grenades were nervously loosened for the hundredth time.

The first sight of one's enemy is a moment that every soldier takes with him to the grave, but none of the Australians had been prepared for the sight that greeted them now as the Japanese suddenly rounded a bend in the road and poured over the bridge. It was a few minutes before 4.00 p.m. and the Japanese came in a column five and six abreast, all riding bicycles and chattering away as though they were out on a picnic expedition.

Behind them, Captain D. J. Duffy, commanding 'B' Company, thought he heard motor transport and he let the first 300 cyclists go through the ambush to be dealt with by the rest of the battalion further along the road. In fact all the noise was coming from three motor cycles which were followed by another 300-400 cyclists. As soon as they were tightly packed in the cutting and on the bridge, Duffy gave the word for explosives which had been laid under it to be detonated.

It went up with a huge blast and bicycles, bodies and debris from the bridge were hurled into the sky. As the explosion went off, the waiting platoons launched their attack, raking the Japanese with machine gun and rifle fire and showering them with grenades. The Japanese, caught completely by surprise, their rifles and automatic guns still strapped to the bikes, were mown down in their hundreds. The only survivors were those who feigned death.

In twenty minutes it was all over and Duffy rallied his men who had withdrawn as planned along Quarry Road and they set off in pursuit of the Japanese who had been let through the ambush. Almost at once they discovered that many of them had turned back after hearing the noise of the ambush. They found themselves face to face with the enemy at bayonet length for the first time. Both sides suffered casualties, but there was no doubting that the Japanese had at last encountered opposition that could hurt them.

Bennett's plan called for heavy artillery fire to be brought down on the Japanese whom it was assumed would be piling up behind the demolished bridge. But the line between Duffy's headquarters and the guns was dead, probably cut by the Japanese who could have seen it beside the road. The battery was in a difficult position because if it opened up at the wrong time it could hit the Australians. In battalion headquarters men strained their ears for the sound of the bridge being blown, but 5 km away heard nothing that would indicate whether Duffy was ready for the artillery.

What they were experiencing was exactly the nightmare that had dogged Heath's troops all the way down Malaya, a breakdown of communications that made it almost impossible to operate with any degree of efficiency. Duffy was not using two-way radio, even though it was available, because there was a strong fear in the services that it allowed the enemy to pin-point their position with great accuracy.

In the withdrawal, Duffy's unit suffered a few casualties. On one occasion they found themselves being shelled by their own artillery, but most of them reported back to battalion headquarters by noon on 16 January.

Tension increased when it was realised at headquarters that the telegraph line with the ambush party had been cut. Although they could hear nothing, they had to assume that the battle had started. Patrols were sent out to try to restore communications and these had several clashes with Japanese coming in the other direction. It was soon discovered that the Japanese had regained control of the ambush area and that Duffy's men had left the scene.

It took the Japanese just six hours to repair the bridge, an extraordinary achievement even allowing for the fact that they found ready-cut timber in a nearby saw-mill. Immediately the advance started again, this time with tanks. Soon after nine the next morning, two tanks arrived at the road block in front of 'C' Company and were sent scuttling under a blaze of fire from the anti-tank guns.

They were followed by three more which fired along the road ahead of them, but they too suffered from the Australian fire. One was set alight and a second disabled and then towed away under fire by the third. Now four more came forward behind the cover of the blazing tank, firing ahead of them, but once more the Australians were too strong. One was hit, another disabled, the third set on fire while the fourth was wrecked by a mortar bomb that went through the turret and exploded.

Then the AIF artillery opened fire on the Japanese troops in the rear. The combined effect of artillery and infantry fire was too much. The Japanese withdrew having suffered heavy losses.

Galleghan chose this moment to launch his own attack, but before it could be started reports indicated that the Japanese build-up of tanks as well as men and artillery had been much faster than he had anticipated. In addition enemy planes were now bombing Gemas and suddenly his own headquarters came under violent attack from dive bombers.

In spite of this new offensive, 'D' Company continued with its advance on a hill occupied by the Japanese about 1000 m from its old position. Galleghan's orders were for it to seize the hill and hold it until dusk before returning under cover of darkness.

'D' Company, under its commander Captain W. S. Melville, was already on its way towards its objective soon after 1.00 p.m. when Galleghan received word that the Japanese, unknown to Melville, were only 300 m ahead of the start line from where he would launch his attack. It was too late to call them back. Almost at the same moment as the news arrived, the company came under attack from ground and air.

The Australians fought bravely, rushing forward and with grenades and bayonets surprising the enemy before being forced to ground by Japanese snipers up trees and by tanks which suddenly appeared.

When they were two-thirds of the way to their objective the fire became so heavy that they were forced to withdraw under cover of fire from their artillery who were now firing over open sights at the Japanese. But the Japanese strength was increasing almost by the minute and the Australians found themselves under attack from seemingly every direction as well as from the air.

AIF ambulances and medical teams went out through the fire to bring back the dying and wounded and the Red Cross symbol was respected by the Japanese who deliberately withheld their fire.

Finally by late afternoon the withdrawal was almost complete. In the two days' action, the Australians had lost one officer and 16 other ranks killed, 9 men were missing and 4 officers and 51 others wounded. Japanese losses were far heavier. The behaviour of the Australians under the most intense fire marked the first reverse the Japanese had suffered since they had landed on Malaya, and proved beyond argument the value of Bennett's vigorous training and strict discipline.

The Japanese noted in their record of the battle that the 2/30th had fought 'with a bravery we have not previously seen'. Indeed it was probably the most effective blow that the Allies struck in the entire campaign, but it had a bitter backlash.

When the news of the ambush reached him, Yamashita immediately altered his plans and decided that he must attack the Australians on the Gemas flank with a wide flanking attack that would take his troops right across to Bennett's Muar front where the weak 45th Brigade was positioned.

Two battalions of the 45th were in position along the winding River Muar supported by the 65th Australian Battery of the 2/15th Field Regiment. The main crossing of the Muar, which was a river navigable to native boats for 160 km upstream from the town, was by ferry across the wide mouth. A network of roads in Malacca converged on this point. Beyond the town, the river flowed through thick jungle so that the defending forces could only man small sections of the banks.

Bennett had been seriously concerned by the gap that was exposed on this west flank through having to leave it in the care of the Indian Brigade, but he had no option with the troops at his disposal. He was criticised for looking on this brigade more as a prospective reserve for his forces inland but had Yamashita not changed his tactics, his assessment would have been unarguable. As it was the Japanese were initially at least untroubled.

They had begun to bomb Muar as early as the 11th but the first troops were only spotted at the northern approach to the ferry on the 15th. They were fired on by the 65th Australian Battery, but the telephone line to the battery's observation post on the far side of the river from the remainder of the Allied forces was broken.

The officer in charge of the observation post disappeared, presumably killed by the Japanese, but his driver, Gunner H. M. M. Fisher, dived into the river and hid all day under the ferry ramp. At nightfall he swam across to the southern bank and was able to supply valuable information to his unit.

As there were no bridges in the vicinity of Muar, the defenders removed all the boats which they thought likely to be useful to the Japanese on the northern bank, and took them across to their own side of the river. That night the Australians poured down 800 rounds of harassing fire, but the Japanese were hardly even delayed.

They went upstream and crossed over the river without being spotted. In the rice fields they found several small boats which the Indians had either not noticed or had not bothered about, and they used these to cross the river further down. Under heavy fire they dragged back to their own side the bigger boats which the Indians had collected. Their losses were heavy, but by dawn they had enough boats to ferry across their entire force. Once the crossing had been made, the untried Indians were no match for them.

They began to pull back in disarray almost immediately, heading for the brigade's headquarters 45 km across country. The Japanese pursued them relentlessly, cutting them down by the dozen and launching blood-curdling bayonet charges on them. They took no prisoners.

Some Australians who were attached fought with great courage at Muar, notably the gunners of 2/4th Australian Anti-Tank Regiment who fearlessly held their ground and destroyed ten Japanese tanks with their fire. Then, when their ammunition ran out, they fought with Molotov cocktails and hand grenades, before being overcome themselves.

In a display of extraordinary courage during the long withdrawal Lieutenant-Colonel C. G. W. Anderson, of the 2/19th Battalion, led many of his men to safety out of an impossible situation. He had also been given command of 45th Brigade after a direct hit on its brigade headquarters had killed or incapacitated almost the entire brigade staff.

An Englishman born in Cape Town, Anderson had been one of the best big game hunters in Africa until he married an Australian girl and moved to New South Wales. He was the man whom Bennett entrusted with the training of the AIF in jungle warfare when they arrived in Malaya and he was an inspiring leader.

When Anderson found himself trapped by the Japanese, knowing that if he did not hold them up Allied defenders at Segamat further inland would be encircled and trapped in the same way, he resisted for a whole week. Then when his men were almost on their last legs, he led them out under cover of darkness right through the lines of the Japanese Imperial Guards, the most elite unit in the Japanese army, and brought them back to safety.

For his gallantry Anderson was awarded the Victoria Cross. Bennett wrote of him in his diary, 'With such coolness, self-control and strength of character and with such kindly affection and consideration of his men, he could overcome all difficulties.'

And Percival, in his book *The War in Malaya* said, 'The Battle of Muar was one of the epics of the Malayan campaign. Our little force by dogged resistance had held up a division of the Japanese Imperial Guards attacking with all the advantages of air and tank support for nearly a week, and in doing so had saved the Segamat force from encirclement and probable annihilation. The award of the Victoria Cross to Lieutenant-Colonel Anderson of the AIF was a fitting tribute both to his own prowess and to the valour of his men.'

There was, however, a horrific postscript to Muar. Anderson had been forced to leave behind 110 Australian and 40 Indian wounded and the Guards herded them into a tiny building and treated them with extreme brutality. Many of the wounded were on stretchers and they were kicked, hit with rifle butts, bayoneted and stripped.

'Many Japanese seemed to delight in kicking where a wound lay open,' one survivor reported, 'and so great was their satisfaction at any visible sign of pain that often the dose was repeated.'

The wounded men were refused food and water, but were taunted with both while the Japanese laughed at their agony in the tropical heat. Then at dusk the Guards tied their captives together, dragged them to the stream and shot or beheaded them. Only a handful, who pretended to be dead, were later able to crawl away under cover of darkness. The atrocity seems to have been in revenge for the escape of the others. Lieutenant-General Takuma Nishimura the Commander of the Imperial Guards Division, was later hanged for the massacre.

After that the concern of the Allies was above all to get to the safety of Singapore as fast as they could. 'The retreat complex is now here with a vengeance,' wrote Bennett in his diary, as climate, disease and demoralisation took their toll.

Wavell, anticipating that the campaign could now have only one conclusion, cabled Percival that, 'You must think out the problem of how to withdraw from the mainland should withdrawal become necessary and how to prolong resistance on the island... Will it be any use holding troops on the southern beaches if attack is coming from the north? Let me have your plans as soon as possible. Your preparations must, of course, be kept *entirely* secret. The battle is to be fought out in Johore until reinforcements arrive and troops must not be allowed to look over their shoulders...make it clear to everyone that the battle is to be fought out in Johore without thought of retreat!'

To Churchill, Wavell sent another signal. 'I must warn you,' he told him, 'that I doubt whether the island can be held for long once Johore is lost.' He had just seen that Percival had still not obeyed his orders to erect fixed defences on the northern coast.

After a conference on the morning of 23 January, Percival gave his orders for the first stage of the withdrawal to the island which he had earlier outlined in a 'secret and personal' letter to Generals Heath, Bennett and Simmons, the Fortress Commander. The withdrawal, a very difficult exercise at any time, was remarkably successful and the Australians found themselves fighting almost every yard of the way back to the causeway. Heavy tropical rain added to their discomfort and Japanese aircraft harassed them constantly, trying to locate and destroy them as they hurried south. Much of the fighting on the ground was with bayonets and bare hands.

As Bennett drove through the ruins of Johore Bahru for the last time, past the abandoned cars and bombed and shelled buildings, he said that he had never felt so sad. 'Words fail me,' he wrote privately. 'This defeat should not have been. The whole thing is fantastic. There seems no justification for it.'

The last of the AIF, the 22nd Brigade who with their artillery had formed the outer bridgehead, were among the last to cross. They said the causeway was so vulnerable that it looked ten miles long. In fact they crossed it in twenty minutes, casting anxious glances at the sky every inch of the way. For some still unexplained reason, General Yamashita, who could hardly be faulted for his conduct of the campaign in Malaya, lost two great opportunities to shorten the war. He allowed reinforcement ships to arrive in Singapore long after he controlled the seas and he made no attempt to send his air force to attack the Allies as they converged on the causeway and then filed across its bare concrete length completely without protection.

The last of the Australians moved on to the causeway at 5.00 a.m. Behind them, with their pipers proudly playing at their head, came the inner bridgehead, the gallant remnants of the 2nd Argyll and Sutherland Highlanders. Last of all, marching ramrod straight, came the Argyll's Commanding Officer, Lieutenant-Colonel Ian Stewart.

As soon as the Argylls were across, sappers and Indian miners fired the huge charge which they had been laying under the causeway for the past several days. Soon after 8.00 a.m. the charges were touched off and the roar of the explosion echoed over the island. When the men looked back, water was racing through a 20 m gap. There would be no more retreat.

Pay Cash,
and Bury Your Dead

The phoney war after the first raid had lasted right through December, but on 1 January 1942 everything had changed. On that day the Japanese launched a savage attack on the city and from New Year's Day until the surrender, hardly a day passed without a raid. How many died in these attacks will never be known. Hundreds just disappeared after some of the raids and hundreds more in the crowded inner city districts were buried in the rubble and never recovered.

For a short time an attempt was made to keep records of casualties, but there was soon no time for paper work. Even the records that were kept disappeared. Officially 600 were killed in January and 1500 injured, but these figures mean little. By the end of the month, 200 were dying each day in Chinatown alone.

For the most part it was continuous rather than very heavy bombing, but the effect on the population was equally devastating. On some days there were nine or ten raids and no sooner had one wave of bombers departed and people emerged from their shelters to start digging in the rubble for their dead and injured or to rescue what was left of their homes, than the alarm siren was wailing again.

The Japanese came in waves of 27, 54 and sometimes even 81 aircraft, usually from the north or north-west. Sometimes they encircled the island to come in from an unexpected quarter. They often used a technique known as carpet bombing, with every plane in the group dropping its bombs simultaneously. The effect of this saturation bombing was gratifying for the Japanese, whose intelligence officers in the city maintained constant contact with the enemy. But it was mainly dictated by the shortage of navigators and bomb aimers in the Japanese air forces.

A squadron's pilots might take all their instructions from their leader, who could be the only fully trained man in the unit, even to the precise moment when they had to let go their bombs.

Edward and Cynthia Koek used to look up angrily to see the Japanese peering over the side of their planes as they passed overhead. There never seemed to be any anti-aircraft guns firing when they were needed. Edward Koek used to say, 'I'm sure if I brought out my gun I could shoot one of those down.' And she would turn on him in mock anger and tell him, 'Don't you dare!' Until in the end they buried his guns, a rifle and a revolver, at the bottom of the garden.

The Japanese used a lot of small bombs which behaved like part-incendiary and part-high explosive. They dropped one on the Koek's garden which infuriated Edward. It killed all their chickens and ducks and broke a few windows, but did little more than that.

These 'pills', as everyone called them, were intended more to demoralise the population and cause havoc in the dense inner-city streets where fire spread so easily, than to cause serious structural damage. Indeed, the Japanese were much more selective in their targets than they had been in Shanghai, for example, where they almost blasted the city to destruction. Their planners had reasoned that they would, after all, only be destroying buildings that they themselves would be occupying in a few weeks.

Almost no one seemed able to grasp that the Japanese advance down the Malayan Peninsula had not been even delayed let alone halted. People *wanted* to believe that Singapore was safe from attack and that the Japanese posed no threat. There were still the half-hearted jokes, no longer even remotely funny as the deadly bombardment continued almost daily, that the Japanese couldn't see in the dark which was why they always carried out their raids by day.

As they sipped their gin slings and *stengahs*, they nodded knowingly and agreed with each other's assessment that as soon as the British and Australians got their new aircraft, the Japanese would be knocked out of the sky. Everyone knew that man for man their pilots were better than the Japanese and nothing ever persuaded them that it was quite untrue.

Meanwhile the gay social life of Singapore went on almost as though war was a hundred years away. From the verandah of the Swimming Club members watched the Japanese raids on the docks with as much detachment as if it had been a matinee at the New World Cinema. While at Raffles the black out had been perfected and the orchestra played for dancers until midnight.

On Sundays curry tiffin was still served by a number of the hotels and the general feeling was that there were adequate provisions for an almost indefinite siege. Nine thousand cattle had been shipped in from Bali and a big dairy herd was brought over the causeway from Johore, supplementing the 125 000 pigs already on the island.

The government did nothing to discourage this belief that Singapore was so well defended that it could never be seriously threatened. Pull up the drawbridge and wait for the reinforcements to come, like the cavalry riding over the hill, was the message and, ostrich-like, everyone believed it. The government from the first day of the landings had embarked on a policy of deliberate manipulation and distortion of the truth and strict censorship was enforced, designed to emphasise the 'growing' strength of the defences even though in most cases they were non-existent.

The troops on the island were often just as confused as the civilians. Singapore Garrison consisted of over 88 000 men who crowded the city's dance halls and Change Alley and frequented the three great amusement centres, New World, Great World and Happy World, which provided everything from restaurants, cinemas and cabaret to seedy dance halls where European and Eurasian 'taxi dancers' could be hired for 25c a dance.

Within walking distance of these *kursaals*, as they were called, were the opium dens and brothels, hidden from more obvious public gaze on government instructions, but there for those who knew where to look.

The island was full of Australian and British soldiers who used their spare time to shop for souvenirs. On the night of the first raid, many of these men had been in town, but almost before the bombs had finished falling, the majority of them were on their way out of town by truck, heading back to their units in case a surprise landing or parachute attack followed the bombardment.

Since 20 December the city had been under martial law, but so powerful was the position of Sir Shenton Thomas as Governor of a crown colony, that he continued to dominate almost every aspect of daily life through his office if not his personality.

He was a good administrator who had spent most of his life in

85

African colonies and he was respected by the Chinese and the Malays who trusted him and believed they could rely on him. In peace time, he would have been — and was — an admirable man for the job, plodding, uncontroversial and dependable. In war he was not a good man to have there, because he was not a very clear thinker and he was complacent and colourless, the last man to inspire the people in a crisis.

He had reached his present position not through any brilliance, but by years of hard work untainted by scandal. By training and temperament he found it difficult to make immediate decisions which conflicted with his stereotyped way of doing things and it was little wonder that he and the army of civil servants whom he controlled sometimes drove the military men to despair.

But the service chiefs, too, were lacklustre and what the people of Malaya and Singapore most needed was a single dynamic figure to take charge and by sheer force of personality rally them against the Japanese. As it was the people of every race were confused and often frightened in spite of the European assurances.

Had there been such a heroic figure in Singapore, that was surely the time for him to emerge, but it didn't happen. The tragedy was that so many people wanted to fight and to prepare the defences, but they were actively discouraged by constant repetition that there was no danger, and even ridiculed when they persisted on their own initiative. At the height of the raids, the volunteer firemen in the Auxiliary Fire Service were jeered and pelted with rubbish by Australian and British soldiers as they hurried to put out a fire.

Had there been the kind of leadership that was needed, the Japanese at the very end of their tenuous supply line and unsure how strong the Allies really were, would have withdrawn. If this had happened, Singapore might have been reinforced before they returned to the attack.

As it was, precious weeks were wasted when nothing was done at all to prepare civil defences for a population that was fast approaching the million mark as refugees from up-country poured on to the island each day.

Almost the only air-raid shelters in the town had been built by the rich, often as gimmicks when there was no perceptible threat to Singapore from anybody. When the raids started in earnest many of these people would not let anyone into them apart from their own families and this caused much bitterness.

There were physical difficulties in building shelters on Singapore.

The surface of the island near the coast was barely above water level so that digging enough large shelters for everybody would have been impossible, and even slit trenches quickly filled up with brine. The few tiny hills on Singapore might have provided some space for shelters, but they were already taken up with Chinese graveyards.

In the city itself there was little room for above-ground shelters, especially in the crowded and inflammable area around Chinatown where they were most needed. There were half-hearted plans for building big shelters above ground level outside the city, but these were always put aside because of the fear that a stampede would follow if quarter of a million people tried to reach them at the same time. And apart from anything else, there were no materials to build them from.

At Duff Cooper's suggestion before he returned home, Brigadier I. Simson, Percival's Chief Engineer and the man responsible for mapping out the military defences of Singapore, was put in charge of civil defence as well. It was a good idea, but they chose the wrong man and demonstrated how difficult it was for any military man to wear a civil hat at the same time.

Simson himself tried hard to have the decision reversed on the grounds that handling Singapore's military defences was more than one man could reasonably have been expected to cope with. His request was overruled.

There were now thousands of refugees on the island who had fled ahead of the Japanese. The treatment they were receiving gave them no encouragement to think that they would be looked after any better in the future. Many of them had fled with only the clothes on their backs and the cash they had in the house, but when they arrived in Singapore there was no assistance for them, no organisation to welcome them and no acknowledgement from the government that they were even there.

The men among them were immediately registered and put to work unless they were too infirm or too old, but the women for the most part were completely ignored unless they happened to have friends on the island which few of the European women did. Often the men were sent out on work parties so quickly that they had no way of telling their wives and families where they were going or how long they would be away.

As the bombing raids increased in frequency and ferocity, these women sometimes didn't even know if their husbands were dead or alive. Bodies were kept for only two or three hours and then, whether they had been identified or not, had to be buried immediately to prevent them becoming a health hazard. With little money and few possessions, and often with small children, the women wandered aimlessly around the city taking cover where they could and haunting government offices for somewhere to live.

In many respects the Europeans among them were worse off than the Asians who had fled with them, for many of these at least had relatives or friends to whom they could turn when they arrived.

Some were more fortunate than others. Those who went straight to Robinsons, for example, and introduced themselves as old customers, received loans that sometimes amounted to hundreds of dollars. The greatest tragedy was that all these women and children could have gone to safety as soon as they arrived, on the ships that were still leaving almost daily. But as part of the Governor's policy of not causing unnecessary consternation, nobody was told that evacuation was even desirable or that London had already authorised the evacuation at government expense of anyone who wanted to go and whose passage had not been paid for them.

In consequence, all through December and January, ships were leaving Singapore for Britain, Australia and India with dozens of empty berths. Most of the women from Malaya as well as most of those who already lived on the island would have welcomed the chance to go.

The presence of many officers' wives and children on the island presented another unexpected problem. As the Japanese danger mounted, they tended to be a potent distraction for their husbands whose prime responsibility should have been to their troops.

Many of the raids concentrated on the waterfront and the airfields, leaving the town relatively untouched. But then without warning, perhaps every sixth raid, the Japanese pilots rained down their terror on the city centre. On one of the worst days, 21 January, a raid on Chinatown killed 383 according to the official figures, but many more than that in reality. And in the same attack, Orchard Road was severely damaged for the first time.

One of the most serious effects of the bombing was that from the start it frightened away most of the city's labour force. It was a problem that was being experienced all over Malaya as workers left their jobs at the first wail of the siren and often did not return until long after the all-clear had sounded.

As the Japanese were coming over up to nine times a day, it

meant that many factories almost stopped production. Within fourteen days of the first raid, production throughout Malaya had fallen by 50 per cent. Even when the city was not the target, the warning was sounded whenever enemy planes were spotted approaching the island.

Within a short time the Army was having to supply its own labour gangs to unload supply ships because the waterside workers were among the first to withhold their labour. This tied up men who should have been used on more important duties.

A large, well-fed labour corps would have been of immense value to the Allies, but every attempt that was made to form such a unit locally failed. The War Council finally agreed, after months of pressure, to labour companies being raised locally, but Sir Shenton Thomas and the Malayan Government opposed it on the grounds that it would interfere with rubber and tin production. The War Council finally destroyed any chance of raising a labour corps by setting a maximum rate of pay that could be offered that was so much lower than the ruling rate that it was impossible to find any recruits.

Percival then went looking for Indian companies without success. Even the Malays, who traditionally expected to work for a pittance, found the rate of pay too low to be attractive. Thomas had the authority to conscript men as labourers, but for political reasons he refused to do this and instead harangued them on the radio. Waterfront workers who stopped work at the first wail of the siren, even before they knew whether the Japanese were approaching the city, and labourers who did not return to work within ten minutes of the all-clear were all lacking in patriotism, he told them. It had no effect.

The few Army labour units that had not fled were being used for repairing the airfields, patching them up after every raid. Even here it was becoming harder to provide each airfield with a full maintenance team and again troops waiting to be sent to the front as reinforcements had to be taken out of vital training to fill the gaps.

The question of whether skilled labour should be used for humbler jobs was another bone of contention. There were many European civilians in Singapore who had engineering qualifications or experience, for example, but who were employed in quite different work, often managerial. The government instigated a campaign to get these people back on the shop floor and this was vigorously supported by the *Straits Times* which said bluntly, 'They should be put to work at their trade without an hour's delay. They must work with their hands. We want no stupid distinctions as to whether a man was a foreman or a director. We cannot all be supervisors and to take up other work merely because there is already an adequate supply of people to control, is positively criminal in present circumstances.'

The most vital need was to find a way of keeping the naval dockyard and engineering workshops open, for these were also responsible for most of the Army's maintenance and repairs. Again, though, the Governor refused to exercise his power to force men to work. Instead he pursued the argument that if the Japanese knew they only had to send one of their planes over Singapore to paralyse work all over the island, they would soon be keeping a plane there permanently. The whole battle to beat the enemy back would be lost because they did not remain at their jobs or go back to the shop floor more quickly.

His plea still had not the slightest effect. As the raids increased, production fell still further and civilian labour, particularly in exposed areas such as the waterfront, was all but non-existent.

The government might have had more success if it had not repeatedly caused intense resentment by some heavy-handed piece of bureaucracy. Typical of this kind of behaviour was the order that it made confiscating every push-bike on the island. It gave no reason and simply acquired tens of thousands of bicycles which then sat in a warehouse until the end of the war to the enormous inconvenience of all those who needed the machines to get to work or visit their families in other parts of the city or the island.

The intention was probably to provide the army with the bikes so that troops could be moved in Japanese fashion from area to area. But there was no co-ordination between the services and the civil administration and once the bicycles were in the warehouse, no attempt was made to take the plan further.

As the raids increased daily and the casualties mounted, the press was in an odd and unsatisfactory situation. Journalists knew the truth of the situation better than anyone. They railed against Sir Shenton Thomas and what they believed to be his dangerous and sterile policy of deluding the population with ridiculous communiques and downright lies. They were rigorously censored

△ Aerial view of Singapore shortly before first bombardment. On the right is the open area of the *padang* with the Cricket Club at one end. (128443)

▽ Victorious Japanese Troops march into Singapore with bayonets fixed. (127906)

△ ARP worker carries a child from a bombed building in Chinatown.
(11529/16)

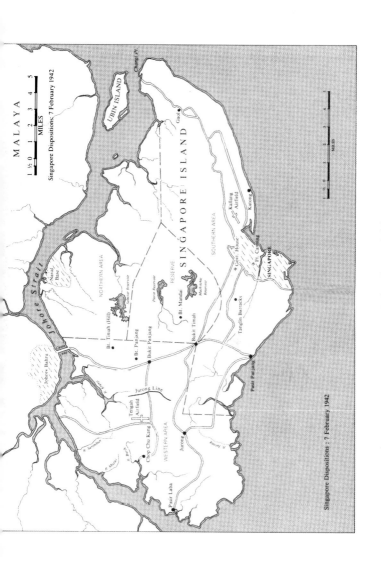

Singapore Dispositions : 7 February 1942

△ Japanese Commander General Yamashita (right), victor of Singapore, later hanged for war crimes. Left is Yamashita's Chief of Staff Lt Gen Susuki. (127913)

△ Lt General A.E. Percival. (7900)

▽ Air Chief Marshal Sir Robert Brooke-Popham (left) with General Sir Archibald Wavell. (128118)

△ Major-General Gordon Bennett. (7094)

△ Australian anti-tank gunners of 8 Division open fire on a Japanese tank. (11302)

▽ ... and the result. (11299)

△ British warship dwarfed in the huge floating dock, Singapore Naval Base. (7748)

▽ RAAF Brewster Buffalos of No. 453 Squadron on Singapore. (100117)

over some matters, like casualty figures, yet were free to criticise the government or the army for their general conduct of the war.

The casualty statistics as well as details of raids on the city and Allied reverses up-country were never given on the grounds that they would demoralise the population. There were stories of fighting overseas and further north in Thailand and beyond, but almost nothing about the war on their doorstep and never any bad news.

Indeed had it not been for the public notices that appeared each day, such as instructions for identifying the dead and the daily appeal for blood donors, people reading the *Straits Times* overseas might have been forgiven for assuming that there wasn't a war going on within 300 km of Singapore. Even those living in the city who could see the raids with their own eyes wondered whether they had been dreaming it all when they read the reports in the papers next day.

The truth was that there were now so many people being killed each day that six centres had to be used to lay them out, including hospitals and one of the pleasure grounds. Public notices gave the procedure for recovering a body and stressed the need for speed: 'The bodies of persons killed by enemy action in the municipal area of Singapore will be removed where possible to mortuaries for a few hours at most where friends or relatives may claim or arrange for their burial if they so wish,' a notice stated. It then added that everyone should wear identification discs at all times so that they could be recognised if they were killed.

Private notices could be inserted in the papers seeking information about missing people, but personal death notices were forbidden on the grounds that long lists of them every day would only depress the public.

In spite of this kind of restriction, the *Straits Times* in particular was a persistent critic of the government. It went about this criticism with candour and regularity, singling out the red tape which strangled almost every initiative that anyone had tried to introduce. Eventually its persistence drew blood, for Thomas, in a remarkable document for a man who was the very quintessence of the career bureaucrat, sent out a circular to every public servant which could serve as a model of its kind even if it was, as the *Times* added ungraciously, two and quarter years late.

'The day of minute papers has gone,' Thomas wrote wistfully.

'There must be no more passing of files from one department to another and from one officer in a department to another. The day of letters and reports is over. All written matter should be in the form of short notes in which only the important points are mentioned of ... Officers who show that they cannot take responsibility should be replaced by those who can. Seniority is of no account.

General MacArthur echoed these words in New Guinea shortly afterwards when he ordered General Eichelberger to replace commissioned officers with sergeants and corporals if they could do the job better.

But bureaucrats do not change their spots overnight and there were many in the public service who continued to stifle any attempt to introduce change or to take account of the very different times in which they were living. A few of them were shipped out of the country, including the Colonial Secretary, a man called S. W. Jones, whose departure was warmly greeted by the *Straits Times* in another leader. The paper waxed quite euphoric when it heard the news that Jones was going.

An official government press release had accompanied the announcement and in the normal course of events this would have been published as a eulogy of what he had achieved in Singapore. The *Times*, however, refused to print a word of it.

'We did not suppress it because of any shortage of space,' it said frankly. 'We did so because publication would have involved a degree of hypocrisy to which we are not prepared to descend. The number of people who will regret the departure of Mr Jones from the office of Colonial Secretary is remarkably few. For ourselves we are prepared to state quite frankly that we have been hoping for it for some time past and welcome it warmly. The only thing we regret is his departure to the United Kingdom.'

What they meant was that Jones should not have been given a free passage back to England and safety but should have stayed and taken his chances in Singapore along with every other public servant and simply been transferred to some other form of work in the defence of the country.

In spite of the daily bombing and shelling, the shops remained well stocked and brightly lit. When the siren sounded, everything closed, but the moment the all-clear was heard, everything returned to normal. Even if some women did have to drive through streets piled high with rubble and littered with corpses, there were usually familiar faces and a friendly greeting when they reached the shops.

'Snappy American frocks for day and afternoon wear' were being advertisied by Robinsons for $12.50 and there were still many luxuries. There was a brisk market for a new 'health' bread which all the bakeries were now being made to bake. 'You must eat the new health bread,' the advertisements insisted. 'No better bread has ever been sold in Singapore before.' The added 'health' came from the Vitamin B which was added to the ingredients.

Food was still in ample supply but hoarding, though not illegal, was actively discouraged. Shop-keepers were instructed not to sell more than two tins of canned food each day to any one person, apart from tinned milk, and some people 'addicted to fancy brands of tea and coffee', as the *Straits Times* put it, were asked not to be annoyed with shop-keepers who refused to sell them their entire stock of a particular brand. In fact, there were enormous stocks of tea and coffee in Singapore, most of which were shipped off to Japan soon after the surrender.

Shops had to stay open for seven hours a day, but they could choose which hours suited them best as long as they were between 6.00 a.m. and 5.00 p.m. on week-days and for four hours on Sundays and public holidays. They had to display a notice outside their shop stating when they would open and the law required them to keep to these hours except in an air-raid and for one hour afterwards.

But the majority of provision stores remained closed between 6.00 and 8.30 in the morning when most people wanted to shop and regardless of when they were supposed to be open. The reason was that the majority of shop owners were profiteering and they could get better prices later than the early morning housewives were prepared to pay.

It was found that prosecutions were impossible to sustain. For the women shopping became an almost insoluble problem. Those who had come down from Kuala Lumpur had encountered the same difficulty there, but it had been at least partially overcome when the government opened several food depots which traded all day and at reasonable prices. This was never done in Singapore.

The Governor, in one of his broadcasts, had a few sharp words for shop-keepers who traded at times that suited only themselves. 'The man who shuts his shop all day,' he chastised them, 'unless he has very good reason for it, is weakening the defence of Singapore.'

At Robinsons in Raffles Place, although business was brisk, credit sales were discouraged, and forbidden altogether for food. Robinsons bought a lot of advertising space in the *Straits Times* to encourage people to send a cheque 'for what you consider the approximate amount due' in settlement of their monthly accounts. Regular postal deliveries — unlike milk deliveries which continued almost to the end — had now been suspended.

The Chinese were more realistic. Immediately after the first raid they abandoned the chit system. Europeans, who since the days of Raffles had never carried money, found themselves without the means of buying basic supplies and food for the Chinese controlled most of the provision shops.

Banks opened between 8.30 and noon, unless air-raids forced them to close, and they continued to trade until the closing days of the fight. A few overseas banks went home clutching their strong-boxes, like the Indian bank which inserted an advertisement in the papers that no cheques on any account would be honoured unless they were presented for payment on or before 21 January when the bank was going back to Madras. The advertisement appeared on 21 January!

The shipping companies, even as late as mid-January, were still doing business although their ships were going out with plenty of berths empty all through the month. P & O offered a first class passage to Calcutta for $185 and second class for $62; and Burns Philp advertised their first class Brisbane, Sydney and Melbourne service for $964 to Sydney and $1000 on to Melbourne. 'First class tickets,' Burns Philp's advertisements noted optimistically, 'are inter-changeable for the return voyage.'

Still many Europeans did not know that they could be evacuated free of charge on these same ships, because the government refused to make any public announcement.

Others were more concerned with selling goods than buying them. Cars which were unlikely to be able to go anywhere within a short time were being optimistically advertised, usually for cash. An Austin Big Seven four-door saloon, black, 32 500 kilometres, in good condition, was offered for $800 cash, but there was nowhere it could go except round and round the island and even the roads there were becoming very dangerous.

Fiercely jingoistic letters were appearing in the press and there were 'authoritative sources' giving fanciful figures to bolster stories of Japanese atrocities. 'Five million civilians killed, 20 million wounded and 1½ million orphaned by the Japanese,' one story in the *Straits Times* ran without comment early in 1942.

There was a brief flurry as people demanded that a cast-iron elephant in front of the old Supreme Court building be turned into scrap for making ammunition to be used against the Thais who were now allies of the Japanese. The elephant had been a gift years before from a long-dead king of Siam. It survived.

Later, after the occupation, a statue of Raffles also survived when the Tokyo-appointed Japanese director of the Museum hid it rather than obey an instruction from Yamashita's anglophobic staff that it was to be destroyed.

A War Fund had been set up to meet some of the costs being incurred by the government in the defence of the island, including the purchase of a fighter. The fund climbed to $6 million, a large part of it a substantial donation from the government itself, and then languished with a brief paragraph in the paper recording each day that ten dollars here and twenty there had been added to it by patriotic citizens.

Crowds of sightseers became as big a problem in Singapore as they are at any disaster and the authorities tried in vain to keep people away, not least for their own safety. 'You must not crowd to a place where a bomb has dropped,' one notice warned. 'The enemy may come back and machine-gun you.'

And another cautioned, 'Do not watch aerial dog-fights. You may be hit by a friendly or enemy bullet fired from many miles away or by pieces of AA shell.' And there was practical advice for those who found incendiary bombs on their property. 'Wait for a full minute before tackling an incendiary bomb.'

An 'Air Raid Alphabet' was compiled and distributed free in several languages, covering everything from 'Buses' ('When the alert sounds, the conductor must stop to allow passengers to dismount if they wish') to 'Parachutists' ('If you see one or two parachutists descending, they are probably our own or enemy pilots baling out. If you see a large number of parachutists, inform the nearest police station at once.')

Drivers had to learn a new set of rules for behaviour in an air-raid. When the alert sounded, all headlights had to be switched off. It was legal to continue driving on side lights, but motorists were advised to stop the car and take shelter after immobilising it. (It was an offence to leave any vehicle, even for a few minutes, without first immobilising it.)

Motorists were encouraged to stop for anyone who looked as though a lift would get them to work faster. 'An empty seat in a car is a waste of petrol—and worse,' was the slogan. 'Maybe there are insurance complications, but we are all taking risks these days and this one is well worth taking. Stop and offer a lift!'

As the Europeans struggled to keep up an appearance of absolute normality, they even convinced themselves in their strange cloud-cuckoo land that the Allied withdrawal back on to the island which had now brought the enemy to the other side of the narrow strip of water which was all that separated them, was a skilful ploy to lure the Japanese on to ground 'that will be more favourable to us'.

They had ignored the stream of refugees who had poured over the causeway even while the troops were withdrawing, the mounting number of dispirited, wounded soldiers in the streets and the incessant bombing that the defending forces were powerless to halt.

The Agony
and Death of a City

In an Order of the Day, Percival had successfully added fear to the existing chaos by dwelling on the 'enemy within our gate' and cautioning against loose talk, although even the most senior officers, let alone any civilians, knew precious little that might be of help to the Japanese and which they did not already know.

Radio announcements and public notices warned people to be constantly on the look-out for fifth columnists of whom there were known to be many in the city; and government-placed advertisements had a drawing of an ear and the caption, 'Don't listen to rumours!'

People were told how to distinguish Japanese from Malays—there was a fear that the Japanese would arrive unnoticed, masquerading in Malay dress—by going up to anyone in the street who looked suspicious and asking them to state their nationality. 'If they try to say "Melayu" (or Malayan), the odds are that they will say "Merayu", because there is no "l" in Japanese.'

Identity cards had to be carried at all times and random house-to-house checks were made to ensure that every occupant had one. To prevent false identity cards being issued, births could only be registered by the mother, or if she was dead, by the father or the child's nearest relative or guardian.

Before the troops began their withdrawal over the causeway, all civilians had been cleared from within a mile of the north coast, so that there was now no way of knowing in the city what was going on on the other side of the island. The first real intimation that they had that the Japanese were much closer than before, was that a new horror was added to the daily bombings, bombardment by artillery.

From the safety of their new positions around Johore Bahru, the Japanese blitzed the city with guns sited on high ground. Using four abandoned airfields in Johore, they now added fighters to the bombers which were causing such havoc. From the day the causeway was breached, casualties climbed to 200 a day killed and countless more wounded.

And now there was another ugly sight in the city. Groups of soldiers and airmen wandered leaderless and without orders through the city streets. Many of them were armed, many were drunk and bullied civilians in the streets and looted at will. There were about equal numbers of Australians and British. The Australian government's representative, V. G. Bowden, cabled his government that their numbers were now so great that they were far beyond the ability of the Military Police to control.

These men seemed to be all over Singapore and there were many more who were neither looting nor drunk, but who had just been separated from their units. Some were exhausted and found rest on the floor of the YMCA. Others, who rejoined their units, found nowhere to sleep and wandered around until they found some means of getting back.

Crème-de-menthe was a favourite drink for the Australian troops who wanted to get drunk, but there were empty and half-finished bottles of every kind of liquor lying in the streets. Much of it came from warehouses that had been smashed open and looted. It was at this time that the volunteer firemen found themselves being jeered and pelted with rubbish by Australian and British soldiers as they hurried to put out fires.

The Cricket Club and Raffles were busier than ever and in every corner there seemed to be people getting quietly or noisily drunk according to their natures. Two of the World amusement parks had closed, but one stayed open and the taxi dancers were in constant demand. Sevenpence bought a roll of tickets that guaranteed you a girl for the rest of the evening.

Stricter food rationing came into force, but the allowance was still quite sufficient and there was a thriving black market. There was still plenty of petrol. Suddenly everyone became civil defence workers so that they could claim an extra petrol allowance.

By 12 February morale was seriously cracking. As Bowden reported back to Australia the increasingly ugly scenes that he witnessed on the streets each day, he heard of a group of

Australians who had boarded a ship without authority and were sailing it to Java. And each time he ventured out, the number of armed Australian deserters seemed to have increased.

After the withdrawal from Johore, the question inevitably arose of whether the military and General Percival should take over control of the city. There had been conflict between the military and the civil authorities since the beginning of hostilities, largely over the question of priorities in Malaya and Singapore.

The military saw their primary task as being the defence of Singapore at any price, while the civil authorities continued to view the strategically important raw materials and the economic strength of Malaya and Singapore as being the first consideration. Certainly Sir Robert Brooke-Popham, the Commander-in-Chief, considered that the Colonial Office put rubber and tin before his need to train men in Malaya and he thought it quite wrong.

Bureaucracies, by their nature, are inefficient machines for fighting wars with and this particular bureaucracy in Singapore had burrowed its way into such a deep rut over nearly a century that it was almost incapable of lifting itself out. But since 20 December, when martial law had been declared, Sir Shenton Thomas had retained almost all the powers and control of the civilian population that he had enjoyed before, and it was clear that a military replacement for him would not necessarily achieve any improvements.

The civil government was still maintaining law and order without difficulty, even if this was largely achieved by lying to the public and inducing them to believe that they had nothing to fear from the Japanese. There were many practical advantages for General Percival in staying well clear of the civilian arena. He and his staff already had their hands full directing military operations and it would have been counter-productive and pointless to try to fight a battle and at the same time run the civil government that was already being efficiently managed and in which he had no experience.

General Gordon Bennett predictably had always advocated the appointment of what he called 'a strong man behind the throne' who would force the civil administration out of its peace-time groove. He had never hidden his contempt for the red-tape bound public servants who seemed to beset his path at every turn.

Percival asked him, apparently only half in jest, if he wanted the job for himself and the Australian replied dead-pan that he would rather be Military Governor. After that, Percival did not raise the matter again.

In fact the *Straits Times* also supported the idea of a Military Governor if Duff Cooper could not stay, 'to cut through the cumbrous procedure which is so hopelessly unsuited to the days in which we live,' as it put it.

Constitutionally the situation was very different in Singapore from that in say Papua or New Guinea where a military commander displaced his civilian counterpart and had him sent back to Australia. Neither Percival nor Brooke-Popham had any authority to do that and they would be most unlikely to get it from London considering the special position of near absolute authority that the Governor of a Crown Colony enjoyed.

The solution was a compromise: Shenton Thomas would look after the civilians, and the military would maintain discipline among its own people and have absolute control of the conduct of the war. If this created a conflict, the demands of the military would have precedence. The system worked surprisingly well right up to the end.

As January dragged into February and the fighting began to spread down the peninsula into the island itself, there was no hiding the growing destruction. The docks were in ruins, large areas of the city had been reduced to rubble and many of the go-downs were empty shells. Orchard Road, the main link between the city and military headquarters at Fort Canning, was again singled out for attack. It also contained the huge municipal market, now almost deserted and eerily lit by guttering candles, as well as the cold storage and many other shops popular with the Europeans.

Burned out and abandoned cars and trucks littered the streets after the raids and bodies lay waiting to be collected.

The city was filled with the debris and refuse of any town under siege and now the Japanese added a new weapon. They dropped millions of leaflets from aircraft, many urging the Asians to turn against the Europeans, or warning them that the Allies were secretly abandoning Singapore and leaving them to their fate. Others described in detail and with crude drawings what would happen to the women in Singapore if it was not surrendered to the Nippon army immediately.

A propaganda programme, was started from Penang radio station designed to break down the morale of the civilians on Singapore which their intelligence sources told the Japanese were still surprisingly high. Over Penang radio they gave a day-by-day schedule which they said they would follow until Singapore had been levelled to the ground and not a living soul was left standing in it. They even included the names of the buildings they would destroy each day and the rumour spread like bush-fire.

When the days went by and the promised damage had not occurred, there was the absurd situation that the people could not even be told. The censorship rules, which prevented any details of bomb damage being reported, prevented the papers from saying where the bombs *had* fallen. This would have immediately given the lie to the Japanese broadcasts. But then censorship still prevented journalists from saying there was a 'front' because that sounded like war; and words like 'besieged' were outlawed because they were considered to be bad for morale.

Few civilians ventured out into the nightmare that their city had become except to buy food and supplies or to cram the docks looking for a way of getting out. A few joined the deserting soldiers who fought their way on board ships leaving for the Dutch East Indies or who hijacked boats and sailed out on their own.

If some of the European homes, with their air-raid shelters and solidly built bungalows, gave a measure of security, the Chinese quarter had no such protection. People went day and night in fear and without sleep. Mass graves swallowed up hundreds of their victims. As the bombing broke more and more sewers and septic tanks and as greater numbers of bodies had to be left to rot in the rubble because there were no labour gangs to move them, the risk of disease increased hourly and the stench in the heat of the day was indescribable.

People learned new lessons in how to cope in the air-raids. They found that some victims were suffocating to death in raids from inhaling dust and plaster, but that covering the mouth and nose with a wet handkerchief reduced the danger.

Others recovering bodies found what one of them described as 'a rather peculiar cloth shoe' on a boy they were pulling out of a bombed house. But as they pulled him clear the 'shoe' fell loose and they could see that it was actually his skin which had been torn away in strips from the calf downwards. The damage had been caused not by the bombs, but by the way he was pulled out as they gradually heaved away the leg from the rubble.

In many cases the dirt that went into these open wounds resulted in gangrene and legs had to be amputated which could have been saved if the victims had been pulled out more carefully. They didn't cry out because by then their legs had been caught in a cramped position for so long that they were completely numb.

Every available building was turned into a makeshift casualty clearing station or hospital. Even St Andrews Cathedral, gleaming with its egg-white and lime, became a first aid post and stretchers and beds replaced pews and chairs. The vestry was converted into an operating theatre.

Edward and Cynthia Koek opened their own centre for the homeless and destitute in the former offices of the Japanese transport group NYK, where they cared for hundreds each day. They had started it on the very first day of bombing and when the raids on the city resumed on New Years Day, they kept it open — 'our little hospital', as they called it — day and night until just before the surrender.

It was not until the end of January that the civil authorities finally made any attempt to co-ordinate and speed up the evacuation of the women and children and of those men who could contribute nothing to the defence of the city and were simply useless mouths to feed.

Even now they still emphasised that the decision to go was entirely voluntary and that there was no compulsion, even for children whom they knew would be in the hands of the Japanese within weeks. And because there was no compulsion, people continued to assume there was no urgency. What kind of government, they asked, would let little children and their mothers stay in Singapore when boats were leaving daily, if there was the slightest danger to them?

And then suddenly — it seemed almost overnight — the real truth dawned on people. There was a wild rush by Europeans to get away from the trap. On 29 January four troopships had arrived with the 18th British Division, the last reinforcements to come. Now these young men sat waiting on the dockside with their piles of equipment, pathetically optimistic about the outcome of a war that was already lost.

It was probably a speech by Churchill which finally triggered the switch for many people and convinced them that all those past weeks, the government had been deceiving them, and that at this eleventh hour Singapore was a very dangerous place for their wives and children to be.

Churchill said, 'We have had a great deal of bad news lately from the Far East and I think it is highly probable we shall have a great deal more. Wrapped up in this bad news will be many tales of blunders and shortcomings.'

The docks and their approach roads had been heavily attacked by the Japanese, but somehow the three remaining troopships escaped damage. Half the big go-downs were smouldering ruins and the smell of burning rubber was acrid in the air. As husbands drove their families towards the dock gates, many had to abandon their vehicles long before the usual boarding place.

There was at least an element of orderliness in the first departures, but this was soon swept to the wind. By the second week in February, those with tickets were fighting and jostling their way up the gangways in their panic to get away, meeting others being forced back to the shore because they had no ticket. Men pushed children aside as they scrambled to make sure they had a place on board for themselves.

P. & O.'s offices had been bombed but tickets were being issued at the manager's house. Europeans who before had disdainfully rejected berths on ships going to India or Australia because they wanted only a direct passage to Britain were grateful to go anywhere.

Passengers were allowed only two suitcases each and ships' crews checked to ensure that no one was trying to smuggle out their pets inside the luggage.

By Friday 13 February, rumours swept the city that no more ships would be leaving. There were heart-rending scenes as wives and children sailed away without a last glance at their husbands who had been stopped at the dockyard gates in spite of the fact that they had passes to leave.

The trauma of having to get a permit to leave and then, at the last moment, being refused permission to do so, was too much for some. They wept openly and tore at the gates, while others screamed abuse at the Chinese police who stood by impassively.

Even in an emergency such as this, the bureaucrats succeeded in making the whole exercise unpleasant and hurtful for many people. Every document required by departing passengers in peace time had to be produced and this particularly affected those Eurasians who had a British father and were therefore entitled to a passage away from the island. Many of them, unable to produce a birth certificate at a moment's notice to prove that their father was

British, were refused a passage on this technicality because they could not satisfy a clerk that they were telling the truth.

There were many sad farewells and many of them turned out to be last farewells. Some of the last ships to leave were sunk by the Japanese, others left husbands behind who would not survive their internment. 'Be a coward,' one wife called across the water to her husband, 'Don't volunteer for anything and just come back!'

And there were some dreadful scenes. A young couple with a baby in the man's arms waited their turn to go through the gates. They had their passes and were on the point of being allowed through when a lone fighter-bomber came in very low over their heads, firing straight ahead of it. The bullets missed them, but a piece of shrapnel struck the wife and killed her instantly leaving her husband standing beside her still clutching the baby and unharmed.

His agony was terrible to see. Beside him lay the body of his dead wife, ahead was the ship that could take him and his baby to safety. A sailor on board shouted to him to hurry up and for a moment he hesitated, weeping, looking down at the body by his feet. The sailor yelled again and the man looked once more at his wife and blinded with tears walked across to the gangway, clutching the baby, leaving the body unburied on the stone wharf.

When there was no longer any doubt that Singapore was going to fall, the banks decided that they must not allow the British currency they held to get into Japanese hands and the only way to ensure this was to burn it. Under the watchful eye of Acting Federal Secretary Eric Petty, $5 million in notes was fed into a furnace. The job took a whole day and there were some good rumours circulating after that exercise.

Not only banks, but businesses and individuals were encouraged to destroy their cash by throwing it into the fire. Cynthia Koek was outside the bank in Raffles Place at the appointed time. 'I think our brains must have been numb,' was how she described it forty years later. 'It was a lovely fire, a huge fire with thousands of dollars all burning gaily and we all dug into our pockets and handbags and just threw any notes we could find on to the pile. Thousands of dollars going up in flames and we couldn't care less!'

Bank officials noted the amount that people were burning and most claims were met after the war.

One other thing that had to be destroyed was liquor. It was an order that was defied by very few for already stories were circulating of the atrocities that had followed in Hong Kong when the Japanese went on a drunken rampage after finding thousands of bottles of drink.

A total ban on all alcohol had come into force on 13 February and wholesalers and retailers were ordered to smash their entire stocks. Customs Department officers broke tens of thousands of bottles that were either awaiting clearance or had been confiscated. Outside one store, a team of six men spent a whole day throwing bottles of spirits and wines against a brick wall. 'I never realised,' one of them wrote rather wistfully in his diary, 'just how long it takes to pull twelve bottles out of a case and throw them against a wall.'

If some lingered a little longer than others at the sacrilege of what they were doing and kept a bottle or two back to ease the long days that lay ahead, the island was pretty well dry by nightfall. Again Cynthia Koek described the bizarre scene outside Robinson's as the store's liquor supplies were systematically destroyed.

'There was a big monsoon drain in Raffles Square in those days, just outside the store and we sat in a row beside it. Then as the men from Robinsons brought out all this drink, we broke the bottles and dropped them into the drain — brandy, champagne, liqueurs, everything. And in the end I began to feel a bit giddy and I said to my husband, "I don't feel very well."

'And he said, "Do you know what? We're all getting tiddly on the fumes!" And do you know, we were! We all got giggly and we couldn't have cared less if there was a war going on or not!'

The *Straits Times* still managed to come out with absurdly optimistic stories that belied the chaos and devastation that was everywhere in the city. After one of the worst bombardments, the paper headlined its lead story, 'Japanese suffer huge casualties in Singapore'.

There were also odd little rousing stories from the battlefront emphasising the ingenuity of the troops which, the *Times* insisted, was helping to drive the enemy back towards the causeway. On 12 February it reported that two Australian infantrymen, one a ventriloquist, had devised a scheme of their own for killing Japanese snipers hidden in the tops of rubber trees.

Four of these snipers had been inflicting a great deal of damage and according to the story, the ventriloquist distracted them by casting his voice while the other man, a sergeant, crept up to the bottom of the trees they were in and shot them from below. All four were killed in this way.

No Europeans in touch with reality doubted any longer that at best their future lay in a Japanese prison camp and at worst in an end that didn't bear thinking about. Those who were resigned to not getting away or who feared, correctly, that the Japanese might be lying in wait for them as they moved into the open sea, made their preparations for going into captivity.

There was a rush on the dentists by people determined not to increase the torment of prison with tooth-ache, and on book-sellers and chemists. Many shop-keepers refused to accept money from their old customers, pressing toothbrushes and soap into their hands with a few kind words and a sympathetic smile. Cigarettes were snapped up, but food was largely ignored, put low on the list of priorities on the assumption that they would have to be fed at least.

The women with young children were a pathetic sight. Many had left it too late to get a berth and had never been told that the government would have evacuated them at no charge; others refused to leave their husbands. Everyone still managed to draw slight comfort from the silly and optimistic communiqués which the government continued to put out.

All that the mothers with children were concerned about now was that they had the bare necessities to keep them alive and healthy. But there was not a single body to whom they could turn for help, not one government or even charitable organisation dispensing clothes and cash for those who had arrived penniless from up-country.

And then, almost in the last hours before the curtain came down in Singapore, there was an astonishing sight. Raffles Place was suddenly filled with excited children in spotless new clothes, the girls in pretty, cool dresses, the boys in shorts and white shirts. All had new sandals and hats and carried a parcel that held a spare set of clothes from underpants to shoes.

This transformation had been brought about, to the everlasting gratitude of the mothers, by Robinson's manager, L. C. Hutchings, who got his board's agreement that all the clothes were to be provided free.

Up at Government House, the Governor, Sir Shenton Thomas, had continued for as long as possible, living much as before. In spite of the heat and the devastation, he insisted on guests wearing collar and tie and his only concession was that they no longer had to dress for dinner.

Lady Thomas was seriously ill with amoebic dysentery and could not even be taken to the air-raid shelter in the grounds. When the Japanese artillery suddenly found the range of Government House at 22 000 metres from their positions outside Johore Bahru, the Governor's ADC used mattresses and bales of wool sent up from the Red Cross to build a makeshift shelter for her under the table in the dining room. A hole just large enough to allow Lady Thomas to be wheeled in on a very low stretcher was the only way in or out.

Several of the Government House staff were killed in the raids—fifth columnists were almost certainly guiding the artillery on to its targets—but Sir Shenton continued calmly with his routine. Every morning his day began after breakfast with the cook bringing him the menu for the rest of the day's meals and when this had been approved he left for his office.

At last the artillery fire was doing so much damage that the Thomas's, she still seriously ill, were forced to leave the house they had sworn they would never be driven from by the Japanese. They moved into the Singapore Club near Raffles Place where they had been given a modest single room for themselves and a second one for the Governor's small remaining staff.

Nearly a hundred other VIPs had crowded into the club and were sleeping four and five to a room. Except for the Governor and his wife, all had to queue up for their meals in a hurriedly converted cafeteria. Lady Thomas was now too ill to eat and Sir Shenton sat on the edge of his bed beside her eating his first emergency meal of bully beef and tinned potato salad washed down with tea and tinned milk.

Outside, across the dying city, the battle raged and Thomas knew that the Japanese were now very close. He anguished over the suffering of his people, Asian and European. He would always argue that his policy of avoiding panic at any cost, if necessary by lying to the population about the dangers that faced them, was the only practical option available to him. And he anguished too over the British, Australian and Indian troops who were fighting a forlorn battle, stalling for time for the reinforcements that would never come.

The Lonely, Frightening Wait

As the last of the 30 000 troops withdrawn from the mainland crossed over the causeway on the morning of Saturday, 31 January, the Australians looked around for the fortifications and defences they had been hearing about for so long. Instead they saw nothing. 'We thought we were coming back to an island fortress where there would be barbed wire and weapon pits and all the paraphernalia of a defended position,' one Australian infantryman recalled, 'and there wasn't a damn thing. Flat beaches and swampy ground and nothing—not even a strand of barbed wire.'

What disturbed them even more was the discovery that the great naval base, which was what they believed they had been fighting to preserve, had not only been evacuated but scuttled. The most visible symbol of British dominance in the Far East was being reduced to so much concrete and metal. When it was most needed, the only time it was ever called on to justify its existence, the base was useless. Many of the men wondered what they had come back to defend when the base lay useless and derelict.

The base had actually been abandoned three days before when the naval staff and European civilians employed there had moved back into the city. From there most of them sailed for Ceylon on one of the ships that had brought the British 18th Division. There had been no other possible course of action once it was accepted that Singapore could not be defended against the Japanese. It was an unpleasant shock for the troops who had watched Brooke-Popham's scorched earth policy being applied all the way back down the mainland, to find the base destroyed even before they had begun to fight for it.

In the strait, to either side of the causeway, an armada of ships, led by two pleasure steamers from the Yangtse Kiang in China, which would have ferried the men across if the Japanese had destroyed the causeway first, began to disperse. Percival's nightmare had been that the enemy would blow the causeway at the last moment and maroon his men on the mainland.

It was ten days since General Wavell had paid his second visit to Singapore and found that his orders for fortifying the northern shores had been ignored by Percival. He had dispatched his signal to Churchill warning him that he doubted whether the island could be held for long after Johore was lost.

In a cable of his own to Churchill, Australian Prime Minister John Curtin pointed out that his government had never expected that Malaya and Singapore might have to be defended without superior Allied sea power. Without a main fleet in the Far East, the forces and equipment available were completely inadequate to meet any major attack by Japan. Australia faced a grave threat and Britain seemed unconcerned.

Churchill replied that he believed it would have been quite wrong to send forces needed to beat Rommel in the Middle East to reinforce the Malayan peninsula when Japan was still at peace; and that no one could have foreseen the speed of events in the Far East or that the British and Americans would experience naval disasters of such magnitude in December. Churchill promised long-term aid to which Curtin retorted impatiently that 'the long distance programme that you outline is encouraging, but the great need is in the immediate future'. This exchange took place a week before the Allies withdrew over the causeway.

Curtin had another cause for anger on behalf of Australia in which he was no more successful. The Australian War Cabinet and the Chiefs of Staff were becoming increasingly resentful that Wavell had not included a single Australian in the top echelons of his ABDA staff. Indeed the most senior job held by an Australian was the relatively minor position of Deputy Superintendent-General in the Administrative Branch.

The Australian Advisory War Council wrote to the Chiefs of Staff in London that the Australian GOC in Malaya, General Bennett, should be given a status that ensured that he and therefore his government was fully consulted in regard to all operational, administrative and other plans that affected the AIF.

Privately, Curtin enjoyed pointing out that Wavell had only won his battles against 'Italians and black troops' in Abyssinia, East Africa and Libya, and that three times when he had come up against the Germans, twice in Libya and once in Greece, he had been defeated. What was more, in Greece the British troops had only been extricated from an impossible situation by General Blamey, the Australian commander.

Wavell, a shy and self-effacing man in spite of his position and reputation (the official Australian historian described him as 'this great commander, perhaps the noblest whom the war discovered in the British armies'), was unmoved. He wrote back offering to appoint an Australian as deputy to his Chief of Staff but no higher; he would however recommend the appointment of an Area Commander within ABDA which would include northern Australia, Ambon and Timor. This commander, he conceded, could be Australian.

It was far less than Curtin wanted, but as events turned out ABDA was so short-lived (it lasted for only six weeks) that no changes were made at all.

During his second visit to Singapore, Wavell had outlined to Percival his orders for the troop dispositions once the men were back on the island. The 18th British Division, he said, as the freshest and strongest formation, should be assigned to the part of the island that was most likely to be attacked; and the 8th Australian Division should be given the next most dangerous sector. He expected them to be very weary when they got back to the island. When the two Indian divisions had been reformed, they should be held in reserve.

Percival told Wavell that he believed the main attack would be on the north-east of the island and that he would therefore place the 18th Division there, with the Australians in the north-west. Wavell disagreed and thought that the attack would be on the north-west in the path of the main Japanese advance down the peninsula, but he accepted Percival's judgement on the ground that he was the commander responsible for results and had studied the problem for longer than anybody else in his command.

Percival then planned his defence of the island in detail. He divided it into three areas, Southern, Northern and Western. The Southern Area, which was the least likely to be attacked, included most of the southern coastline as well as the city of Singapore itself and an area that extended out to Changi in the east. It would be commanded by the Fortress Commander, General Simmons, who would have the Fortress troops, the fixed defences, two Malayan infantry brigades and the Straits Settlements Volunteer Force, a patriotic, but only scantily trained unit. The two Malayan brigades included battalions from three British regiments, the Loyals, Manchesters and Gordon Highlanders. The airfield at Kallang was defended by two battalions of the Indian State Forces.

Immediately to the north of the city was the Command Reserve, the 12th Indian Infantry Brigade which consisted of only two battalions. There were 400 men of the Argyll and Sutherland Highlanders, including 150 marines and 400 half-trained Indians of the 4/19th Hyderabads.

General Heath and his III Indian Corps were in the area to the east of the Bukit Timah Road, which was confusingly called the Northern Area. Their main strength was the newly arrived 18th British Division.

Practically all the western half of the island, including the approaches to the causeway, was entrusted to the 8th Australian Division and was known as the Western Area. The 44th Indian Division was also attached to the Australians.

The three commanders were allowed to keep only one battalion each in reserve.

Percival's plan was to occupy the fringe of the island where he would attempt to hold the Japanese as they were crossing the strait in their boats. They were tactics that would have stood much more chance of success if there had been enough troops available to cover the whole front with rifle and machine-gun fire and if there had been some way of lighting the whole front during the night when a landing was most probable.

In fact there were not enough troops and the Australians were spread so thinly on the ground (two battalions of the 22nd Brigade, for instance, had to defend nearly 14 km of shoreline) that in many places the defences were little more than outposts of a few men dotted along the coast. Because of the terrain of swamp and mangrove, they were often not even in contact with the section next to them.

In spite of this, Percival had few other options with the forces at his disposal and he had anticipated the problem in a secret letter dated 23 January in which he had outlined his plan for the defence of the island. He had said in this letter that the shores in Bennett's and Heath's areas particularly were too intersected by creeks and mangrove swamps for any recognised form of defence. The general plan in each area would therefore include small defended localities to cover the known approaches, such as rivers, creeks and roads to the coast, or tracks along which vehicles could travel. He added that these localities would be supported by mobile reserves which would operate against any enemy parties that tried to infiltrate in the intervening country.

Percival gave orders that apart from preparing immediate defensive positions and clearing fields of fire, no defensive work was to be carried out by the troops in the three areas. But for the first time, the Fortress Commander, General Keith Simmons, did begin to take steps to prepare fixed defences and more was done in the following week after the withdrawal on to the island than during the previous year.

The AIF had no prepared positions in their sector except for a small plot at Pasir Laba in the south west which protected the western entrance to the strait. There a small company of the Malay Regiment was protecting two 6-inch guns, two elderly 2.7-inch howitzers and two even older 18-pounders.

In terms of difficulty in setting up an effective defensive position, the Australians had by far the hardest task and when Percival inspected the AIF's lines soon after the men were in position, he agreed with Bennett that the Australians' area would be difficult to hold with so few troops. Once the Japanese were ashore in large numbers, there would be no more chance of containing them than there had been on the mainland. Percival must have agreed with Bennett who wrote in his diary, 'I realise the unfairness of asking men to fight with such meagre resources.' But the only way out of that predicament was more soldiers and of these there were none.

The two Australian battalions which had fought at Muar were so depleted that the 2/29th took in 500 reinforcements when it arrived back on Singapore and the 2/19th another 370. Of the 2/29th battalion's company commanders, only one survived the Muar action and 19 new officers, mostly from reinforcements, had been appointed to the battalion.

Colonel J. H. Thyer, a Signals Officer who had become an expert in infantry tactics and Bennett's GSO1, or senior staff officer, later described the quality of these reinforcements. 'Of those allotted to the 2/29th Battalion the great majority had arrived from Australia as late as the 24th of January... Some had sailed within a fortnight of enlistment. A large proportion had not qualified at a small arms course nor had been taught bayonet fighting. Naturally they were ignorant of the conditions in Malaya or elsewhere... some reinforcements to all battalions had never seen a bren gun and none of them had handled a sub-machine gun or an anti-tank rifle. Worse still was the fact that there were some who had never handled a rifle.'

There was no time to give the men the training they needed — at least three months in the opinion of Brigadier Maxwell, the commander of the 27th Brigade. Bennett could do no more than arrange for them to have some basic training so that they could at least fire a rifle.

Bennett had also pointed out to Percival the inequality in the size of the areas that the Australians and the 18th Division had been given. The 18th were in easier country and had a much shorter frontage to protect and although Percival agreed, he said that he was still convinced that the Japanese would land on the north-east and so encounter the 18th. (Though once again Percival contradicted himself later. When he was writing after the war, he gave a completely different account of events to those he had given to Wavell and Percival, claiming that he too had been expecting the Japanese to land in the north-west, as they did.)

One can only accept Percival's version of events at the time and not as he chose to remember them later. There was no question in anybody else's mind that he had expressed the opinion that the most dangerous area was the north-east. If his later version is right, and he really did believe that the Australians would be attacked first, then he was disobeying Wavell who had specifically told him to position the 18th in the area where the Japanese were most likely to cross.

Presumably in line with the north-east theory, by far the greatest strength of artillery was allotted to Heath's Northern Area — five field artillery regiments, two anti-tank regiments and one mountain regiment in addition to its three fixed batteries. The Australians eventually received only three field artillery regiments and three anti-tank batteries in addition to the one fixed battery at Pasir Laba.

This allocation to Bennett's area meant that less than 5 per cent of its three-brigade frontage could be engaged by his artillery at any one time, and only about one seventh of the front could receive its support at one time.

What artillery there was would have been more effective if Malaya Command had not ordered its ammunition to be strictly rationed. Anticipating a three-month siege, Percival had ordered that except in immediate attack or defence, the 25-pounders were not to use more than 12 rounds a day, the 18-pounders 25 rounds and the howitzers 29 rounds. The gunners were not allowed to accumulate these allocations or even to transfer them from gun to gun if one battery found itself with more targets than another. The restrictions effectively prevented any training, so that when the artillery was used, it was much less accurate and effective than it could have been.

The frontages along the coast were allocated down to brigade level by General Keith Simmons, the Fortress Commander, and his staff. Among them was Major C. B. Dawkins, Bennett's GSO2 or second most senior staff officer.

The River Kranji, 1200 m wide where it reached the Johore Strait west of the causeway, was a natural boundary in the northern part of Bennett's area. Simmons placed the 27th Brigade east of the river and across to the causeway and the 22nd Brigade west of it on a front that extended right down to the River Berih about half way down the west coast.

This meant that the 22nd had a frontage to the strait of about 16 000 m compared with the 27th's 4000 m, in spite of the fact that the 22nd's frontage was closer to the mainland. The 2/29th battalion of the 27th Brigade, which had so many raw recruits that its efficiency was very suspect, was the reserve unit and would go to the aid of either brigade.

The 44th Indian Brigade was given the south-west sector of the Western Area. Although it had an even longer frontage of 21 000 m from the Berih right round to the Jurong, it seemed to be less immediately exposed to attack.

Bennett sited his headquarters on the Jurong Road, about 1300 m north-west of Bukit Timah village. It was a considerable distance back from any likely landing area by the Japanese, but it gave Bennett rapid access by road to any of his brigade positions.

The unit patrolling the swamps and open spaces behind the AIF was a strange force of Chinese irregulars commanded by a Lieutenant-Colonel J. D. Dalley of the Federated Malay States Police Force. They had been recruited from all classes of Chinese: college boys and rickshaw pullers, loyalists and communists, old and young, as Percival described them. They were armed with an assortment of shot guns, air rifles, service rifles and pistols. Later Dalforce, as they became known after their commander, became the centre of the resistance movement in Malaya and the most hated of the adversaries of the Japanese. They were extremely tough and brave, but almost totally untrained in Singapore which reduced their efficiency to the point where one Australian officer who knew them well described them as little more than 'a motley crew'.

When they came off the causeway, the 22nd Brigade had to march past the 27th which was already preparing its positions in what had become known as the Causeway sector, as they were driven round to the far side of the Kranji to their own positions. To meet Percival's requirements for defending the beaches, each of 22nd's three battalions had to cover a frontage of about 5 km. The 2/20th with a machine gun platoon and a company of Dalforce was on the right, with a frontage of 8000 yards from the Kranji to a point near the River Sarimbun on the west coast; and the 2/18th was on the left between the Sarimbun and the River Murai, also with a machine gun platoon.

The 2/19th Battalion was positioned by Brigadier Taylor with a machine gun platoon so that it covered the coast from the Murai to the Berih and the Choa Chu Kang road. The brigade was now left without a reserve battalion, but each battalion had to hold one company in reserve in its headquarters area.

The Tengah airfield which was in the brigade's area was guarded by units of the Jind Infantry Regiment, one of the better units of the Indian State Forces.

The 44th Infantry Brigade, commanded by Brigadier G. C. Ballentine, also had all its battalions of Punjabis in forward positions to guard their long frontage. As at Muar, Bennett found his left flank occupied by raw, almost untrained Indian troops. The frontage from Ballentine's left battalion right round to the causeway consisted of an almost continuous fringe of mangrove swamps.

Brigadier Maxwell, who had the shortest frontage of the

Australian units, positioned his 2/30th Battalion near the entrance to the causeway; the 2/26th to the left of the 2/30th, covering the coast and the mouth of the river; and the 2/29th in reserve. Maxwell, however, was very concerned about the southern part of his sector which extended 8 km back from the beach and which he believed could be penetrated by the Japanese if they broke through the Indians on the other side of the causeway or landed on the east coast and made a forced march across country. The 2/29th was therefore given the additional responsibility of protecting the brigade's rear.

Over in the west, the 2/19th felt so separated from the other two battalions that several members after the war believed incorrectly that they had been in reserve. They were put into a rubber plantation and in the plantation factory, where the latex was cured, they found a lot of heavy timber boxes. As in most places on the island, they could dig down only about 600 mm before the water began to seep in. They piled the earth up in front of their slit trenches and then put these boxes on top, finally covering them with soil. It gave them some overhead protection and saved many lives for nobody brought them any barbed wire or other materials.

Most of the week following the withdrawal was spent digging in and preparing positions. The weather held out for them and apart from the occasional afternoon downpour, conditions were quite good. It was well that they were, because many of the Australians were suffering from diseases and sores picked up during the appalling monsoon weather and conditions in which they had been fighting on the peninsula. Tinea and tropical ulcers were common and the men who had fought on the mainland were, as one of them put it, 'a pretty horrible mess from the waist down'.

Several of them had malaria and it was common for sections which normally consisted of ten men to be reduced to seven or even six.

At least one doctor, now a consultant physician, believes that malaria played a far more significant role in the Allied defeat than is normally accepted. Quinine was quite freely available to both sides during the war, but quinine, as this doctor points out, is a malaria preventative and not a repressant. Once you have the disease, it is of very limited use.

The Allies had no repressant and therefore no way of alleviating the debilitating symptoms of the disease, but the Japanese did.

They had received from Germany ample stocks of a most effective malaria repressant. In consequence they were far less troubled by the symptoms of the disease than were Percival's troops. 'It is not an exaggeration,' says the doctor, 'that on some days the effect of this would have been like sending the Australians into fight with one arm tied behind their backs.'

The irony was that the British had known that the repressant had been available in France since the outbreak of war, but nobody had thought of sending any to Malaya or Singapore.

Tropical ulcers, which became one of the scourges of life on the Death Railway, troubled many, but in Singapore they rarely kept a man off his feet. The medical officers had orders that nobody was to be evacuated who could still walk.

Digging in proved too difficult in many places where the water began to ooze through almost before the shovel had turned the top layer of sand. The only answer when this happened was to build upwards with breastworks which at least protected the body from the shoulders down from rifle and machine gun fire.

As the men dug or built, the padres who had met them at the end of the causeway with coffee and cigarettes, a change of socks and a friendly word, tried to keep their spirits up. Some were buoyed by the realisation that whatever the outcome of the battle, the exhausting ritual of fighting, withdrawing, fighting and withdrawing again, until they were so exhausted they could hardly put one foot in front of another, was finally over.

Even if their immediate area was not the heavily defended fortress they had been expecting to find, they still assumed that there were unlimited supplies and ammunition further back in the rear which would allow them to resist a siege until the new reinforcements arrived which they had always been promised.

They settled down in their cramped, uncomfortable positions and waited, straining their ears for the first whispered order, the first splash of oar blades on water that might signal the start of the last stage of this hateful war. The night was always frightening in the jungle and for the waiting Australians every shadow on the strait became a landing craft, every cracking twig a Japanese patrol creeping up behind them. A hundred times they imagined what it would feel like to have cold steel thrust hard into their bellies, to push their own bayonets deep into a Japanese, then twist and pull out. The night was no time to have an imagination.

They sat in their lonely outposts, usually two in each defensive position to give each other moral support, and talked softly to keep those imaginations from running riot. They knew that Percival expected the Japanese asault to be on the other side of the island, but that Bennett believed it would come on their side. Wherever it happened, they wished the Japs would get on with it.

When Gordon Bennett got back to his bungalow after the inspection of the Australian lines with Percival, he settled down to read the day's signals. He had just made himself comfortable when bullets began crashing into the walls of the house. In seconds he was on his feet and racing to put out the lights, and then just as suddenly as it had started, the firing stopped.

He waited for a few minutes, but it didn't resume, and he went cautiously out to find out what had happened. To his considerable surprise, a servant who was the only person around seemed entirely unconcerned and after a short time he was able to establish what had happened. The air-raid wardens in Singapore, whose territory extended some distance out of the town centre, had found an effective and time-saving method of making householders observe the black-out, or brown-out as they called it. When they saw a light, they opened fire on the building. It somehow seemed very prophetic.

Into the Killing Area

The Japanese had begun planning the detail of the final assault on Singapore immediately after the capture of Kuala Lumpur. They now knew the strength or lack of it of their enemy and they could draw up a time-table with considerable confidence. It was planned that the attack would be launched on 7 February, although Yamashita postponed this later by twenty-four hours to give his commanders additional time to prepare.

The Allies had withdrawn so quickly down the peninsula that some XXV Army planners believed that Percival would either surrender Singapore very quickly or would try to get as many of his troops to safety as he could without attempting any full-scale defence of the island. To counter such an evacuation and to cut off any more convoys bringing in reinforcements, Japanese warships and submarines were sent to lie in wait off the south coast of the island. They attacked vessels entering and leaving. One of the four ships bringing in the 18th British Division had been set on fire and sunk.

Others at Japanese headquarters, however, believed that the British would fight stubbornly, possibly to the last man, and among these was the Chief of Staff, General Susuki, who was in charge of the planning. Susuki, on the other hand, did not believe that Percival was a man who would expose Singapore's huge civilian population, now in excess of one million with the flood of refugees who had arrived from the mainland, to a blood-bath that would cause them untold suffering without altering the outcome of the battle. He could sympathise with Percival whom he knew must be trying to work out some effective defence around a battlefield cluttered with a million civilians.

Whichever policy the British general adopted, it was clearly important for the XXV Army to act quickly and to throw as heavy a force as possible against the island. Susuki's intelligence sources were still good and Japanese spies on the island provided him with a stream of information right up to the end. There were in addition almost certainly collaborators among the Malay and Indian troops who slipped messages back to the city about troop dispositions from where they were relayed across to Johore.

The one vital piece of information that Yamashita never had was the actual total strength of the Allied defending force. He constantly over-estimated it, as Percival also would over-estimate the strength of the Japanese.

Yamashita was not concerned by the strength of the Australian and British defences on the north coast. He knew that these would be easily crushed, either by his artillery or by the first wave of landing troops, and the only question that had to be resolved was on which side of the island he would land his men.

Pre-war plans for the capture of Singapore show the assault on the north-west coast where the Australians were now positioned. The strait is narrowest on that side and the Japanese would be in their element fighting in the jungle and mangrove that went almost to the water's edge. As Wavell and Bennett had foreseen, the roads on the other side of the water would greatly simplify the assembly of troops and equipment for an assault on the north-west. There were also numerous rivers and streams on that side of the Johore coast where the Japanese could hide their landing craft.

Susuki's planners, however, opted for a three-pronged attack along a broad front extending from a point east of the naval base and then right along the Johore Strait to the western side of the island. But when his intelligence reports revealed the strength of the force that Percival had put into his Northern Area, Susuki went back to the original concept of concentrating on the north-west. At no time did he contemplate, as Percival anticipated, a concentrated landing on the north-east coast.

By 4 February Yamashita's artillery was in position in the south of Johore and it at once began lobbing shells into the Allied positions. Ranging shots were quickly followed by a full-scale bombardment and their first targets were the three northern airfields which were quickly evacuated by their Indian defenders. After these they concentrated on oil installations, road junctions and Allied artillery positions.

Soon afterwards a long-range gun was pulled into position and began lobbing shells 20 km into the heart of the city. At the same time Japanese aircraft bombed and strafed almost with impunity for the few aircraft that Air Vice-Marshal Pulford had left were no match for the Japanese. Their main targets were the water supply, the supply dumps and the airfields, as well as the Chinese quarter and other residential areas.

The big 15-inch guns of Johore Battery at Changi Point on the eastern tip of the island were attacked, but they at least escaped serious damage.

Percival's artillery replied half-heartedly, but the Japanese firing was so accurate that he was afraid of disclosing the location of his fixed positions if he used their guns. Most of the artillery fire on the island when the Japanese began their bombardment was carried out by mobile field artillery sections, but these were among the guns restricted to firing no more than twenty rounds a day, so that the damage they could do by the time they had found their range was very limited.

The Allied anti-aircraft guns were a prime target for the Japanese gunners and pilots who could now strike the island whenever and wherever they chose.

Under cover of the bombardment the Japanese began to prepare for the attack in great secrecy. For the assault they assembled an armada of 300 landing craft which they concealed well upstream in the rivers and creeks that flowed into the north-west arm of Johore Strait and where they were out of sight of any Allied patrols.

To ensure that their movements were not betrayed, they cleared all civilians out of a 20 km strip along the strait and then assembled the 5th and 18th Divisions which would be making the assault well back in the jungle where they could not be seen from Singapore Island.

Engineers reconnoitred Johore Strait, checking tides and depths and a patrol slipped across to Singapore to look at Percival's beach defences and obstacles, perhaps passing the Allied patrols crossing the water for their own purposes.

The Japanese flotilla included 200 collapsible motor boats which could carry a dozen men or a field gun; 60 motor-driven pontoons which could be used either for carrying 20 men or for bridging; 7 heavy pontoons for transporting trucks and tanks; and 30 small landing craft which could each carry 36 troops. It was a formidable task force.

To maintain secrecy, most of the landing craft were brought down to southern Malaya in sealed railway trucks while the motorised barges came down the west coast by sea from Port Swettenham, Kuala Lumpur's port. When they were near Johore Strait, the Japanese carried the barges the rest of the way overland for greater secrecy. For three days their engineers then worked on the boats in the Muar River to ensure that they were familiar with them. Most of the infantrymen who would take part in the landings were already trained assault troops with experience of river crossings and amphibious operations, and rehearsals were deliberately kept to a minimum.

They took the same care preparing the artillery and Susuki's plan was to take across 168 guns with much more ammunition than normal — 1000 rounds for each field artillery gun and 500 rounds for each of the heavy guns. The divisional artillery moved into position to support the assault units, while the Army artillery took up positions on top of the highest ground in southern Johore which was a hill north-east of Johore Bahru. These were the guns which were firing with such devastating effect on the island and which could blast away with impunity at any part of the island.

The artillery was ordered to destroy the Allied oil tanks on Johore Strait before the assault started to prevent Percival from draining the fuel into the water and then setting it on fire to turn the strait into a burning death trap. By the time the week was out, they would wish that they had carried out this task more thoroughly.

The air support provided by Army Air Force planes included only eight bombers, forty fighters and fourteen reconnaisance aircraft but this was considered more than adequate as there was no serious opposition from Pulford's air force or even from the anti-aircraft guns.

The strict rationing of ammunition ordered by Percival had some absurd consequences for the Australians. They had to wait for more than twenty-four hours before they were given permission to fire at the tower of the Johore Bahru administration building which they could see through their binoculars was being used by the Japanese as an observation post. It was a target that did not come strictly within Percival's guide lines. Eventually they were given permission to fire at it and they damaged the building substantially, driving out the observation post.

After that the Japanese sent their observers up in a balloon which floated frustratingly just out of range of small arms fire and from which they had a bird's eye view of the island and what would soon be the battle-field.

The Allies meanwhile continued with their own preparations under almost continuous fire. They had a ten-day reserve of ammunition and supplies, but the Japanese air and artillery activity was so fierce that supplies could only be moved after dark and the only men available to do the job were the troops themselves. They worked on their positions all day, constantly under fire, and then moved up supplies at night until they were weary and run down through lack of sleep. The remnants of the Labour Corps were useless under fire and civilians who might have been brought in had all been evacuated 1.6 km back from the beaches.

The location of the supply dumps and depots was another cause of growing concern for Bennett and Heath in particular. Most of them had been sited in positions where they could support guns and troops repelling an attack from the sea and they had been widely dispersed to give them greater protection against air attack. Some were in the middle of the island while others, including important ammunition magazines, were in the Northern Area and would quickly fall to the Japanese if they landed. All were about as inconveniently placed as possible for the Australians on the far side of the Kranji.

If Percival had taken the proper steps to install the fixed defences that General Wavell had ordered, these supply positions would have been relocated. But by the time the gravity of the situation was realised it was too late.

The Australians to the left of the causeway continued to improve their positions while artillery fire poured down on them or went over their heads. Casualties were small, but the constant bombardment was demoralising and made even the simplest tasks hazardous and difficult. Even the endless struggle to keep their weapons and ammunition dry was made more tedious when every shell opened up another water-filled crater and there was spray everywhere.

Percival urged his commanders on to complete their positions because he was sure that Yamashita would attack as soon as he was ready in order to free his troops and planes for other operations in the Far East. He had not entirely dismissed the possibility that the Japanese would launch a simultaneous attack from the sea, either from the Anambas or through the Strait of Malacca; or that there would be a landing by airborne troops to win possession of the airfields and possibly his own headquarters. He had correctly judged that Yamashita would use three divisions for the assault and keep more troops in reserve.

With his forces already stretched to the limit, there was nothing he could do to prepare for either a naval bombardment and an amphibious assault on the south or east coasts, or to defend against an airborne landing, for his troops were already spread so thinly that in places he knew they would be ineffectual.

The last reinforcement convoy had arrived, bringing with it the units of the British 18th Division and a few Indians, and most of the men on board the ship that had been attacked and set alight had been rescued. Almost all their weapons and equipment however as well as the guns of an anti-tank regiment had been lost.

On paper Percival could match the Japanese strength with the near-100 000 men at his disposal. But this was only on paper for only about 75 000 of them were combat troops. The majority of the rest were unarmed base-line troops. The 41 battalions that remained were in a pitiable state with morale at a low level and many of their members sick or in hospital. (Thirteen of the battalions were British, six Australian, seventeen Indian, two Malayan and three others.).

On average he now only had ten fighters in the air each day, all out-dated and out-classed by the Japanese. The best the pilots could do was take off and fight bravely and hope that they get safely back to land. The Japanese artillery fire and bombing had been so heavy that Kallang was now the only airfield operating and it was a constant struggle to maintain even this in a condition that would allow the fighters to operate.

Percival sent out patrols each night but inexplicably could find no heavy concentrations of Japanese troops, which of course had been hidden inland from the coast by Yamashita. He therefore wrongly assumed that the attack was not yet imminent.

The first sign of activity was a sudden flurry on the mainland opposite the naval base and the Japanese began to put up a camp.

Soon afterwards their Guards artillery started to fire at targets on the north-east coast.

Percival was confused even though the Japanese action seemed to confirm the accuracy of his prediction that they would make their assault on his north-east coast. But his confusion was part of an ingenious Japanese scheme, for all this activity was nothing more than a complicated diversion intended to syphon troops away from the other side of the causeway where the genuine landing was to be made. Each evening long columns of trucks drove eastwards, their headlights flashing to draw them to the attention of the watching troops across the strait, their engines growling in low gear to give the appearance of a heavy load. In fact they were all empty.

On the night of Saturday 7 February the Imperial Guards Division — the same unit that had massacred the wounded Australians and Indians at Muar and which had been responsible for the diversion opposite the naval base — landed a 400-man detachment on Ubin Island in the eastern mouth of Johore Strait. Its purpose was to reinforce the idea that the Japanese were preparing a major landing on that corner of Singapore Island. The British patrols and observers on Ubin withdrew immediately and the Japanese placed their light artillery in a position from which it could inflict maximum damage on the main island.

The primary purpose of the exercise, to draw troops away from the other side of the island, failed, not because Percival was not taken in by it, but because he had already positioned as many men as he could spare in the north-east. Meanwhile, all through the nights of the 6th and 7th, the Australians at their end of the island could hear the sounds of hammering and chopping on the mainland and they were convinced that whatever was going on opposite the naval base, an attack on their front was only days away at most.

On the night of the 6th Brigadier Taylor sent three patrols across to Johore. He personally watched them slipping away into the darkness. The first was spotted by the Japanese and attacked with hand grenades as it approached the opposite shore. The patrol leader was killed and the boat sunk and the others were fortunate to be able to swim back to safety.

The other two patrols landed without incident and stayed behind the Japanese lines for twenty-four hours. For the first time they found large concentrations of troops a short distance inland and on high ground, but to their surprise there were no landing craft even though there were plenty of vehicle movements. They had not gone far enough upstream to find the boats hidden in the reeds and when they reported back to Percival, he was again convinced that the time for the landing had not yet arrived.

That same night other Australian troops sank a boat carrying thirty Japanese soldiers, probably a sabotage party sent to destroy the oil installations, as they crossed the strait just west of the causeway.

Finally, early on the morning of Sunday 8 February, the Japanese began their final softening-up bombardment that would go on relentlessly all that day and well into the evening. Japanese planes stepped up their attacks on the coast, concentrating on 22 Brigade defences and trying to knock out its guns and searchlights.

They had opened up as usual with a few ranging shots, lobbing them nonchalantly on to the 2/20th Battalion in its position on the beach. By 9.30 a.m. the brigade's first casualties were being brought in. By dawn the next day, the battalion had lost nearly 550 of its 1100 men, with 330 of them killed.

The first Australian casualty was a big man called 'Brick' Bradford of the 2/20th and the stretcher bearers brought him back through the lines with both his shins chopped out by a bomb that had burst above him. Many of the men had never seen a battle casualty and the sight of this big man lying helpless and in agony brought home to them, as even the bombardment had never done, the harsh reality of the war they were fighting.

The stretcher bearers carrying him back to the Casualty Clearing Station found that to reach it they had to get past a place where the British had begun to gouge out a landing strip, about 500 m long and 100 m wide, behind the Australian lines. The trees had been bulldozed, but the ground was still as rough as a ploughed field. With the choice of either going the long way round the strip or risking being caught in the middle if they went straight across, they took the gamble and were half way across when a Japanese fighter came straight down the clearing at tree-top height.

The pilot came the whole way down the strip and Bradford was calling out to them to leave him while they just stood there 'like bloody shags on a rock', as one of them said afterwards. But the pilot turned without firing, made a big circle and came in a second time as though he was trying to line them up in his sights. But again he buzzed them and made no attempt to fire. There were many such incidents when Japanese airmen — and occasionally ground forces — were chivalrous enough not to fire on a stretcher party, but those bearers never took that short cut again.

They got Bradford back to the clearing station where doctors removed one of his legs. He lived and went on to survive three years imprisonment in Changi.

By the time the stretcher bearers had got back to their position on the beach, the 2/20th was under even heavier fire than when they had left and two more casualties were lying in a trench waiting to be evacuated, both from the machine gun platoon. One of the men, wounded almost beyond recognition, was cursing in his dying breaths every Jap who lived.

The ration truck arrived in a brief lull in the firing, but as though suddenly spotting it the artillery on Johore opened up with a new burst of fury and the men dived for their trenches or breast-works, grabbing any tins within reach. Some had to make do with cold tinned potatoes for the rest of that day.

The Casualty Clearing Stations passed the wounded with more than superficial injuries back to the 10th Australian Base Hospital which had been set up in a Methodist school half-way along the Bukit Timah Road. Beds had been prepared in the dormitories and a large marquee erected in the grounds where all new arrivals were taken.

The flood of casualties began within an hour of the bombardment starting and the medical teams worked like robots while aircraft screamed overhead and one-ton shells from the big 15-inch guns roared past like a train on their way to Johore. Occasionally an artillery shell burst close by and the whole building shook. It was exhausting for the doctors and nursing staff and nerve-racking for the wounded.

As the day wore on the onslaught on the Australians became even fiercer, if that was imaginable, until the artillery fire sounded like drum-rolls and the noise was overwhelming. Men who had been under attack in World War I had never experienced such fire. For most of the afternoon it was too dangerous even to lift their heads above ground and the men of the 2/19th, back in the rubber plantation, had reason to be grateful for the overhead shelters they had made from the packing cases which saved their lives time after time. Many Australians who had no boxes to cover themselves with died under the artillery fire.

In fact the number of casualties was comparatively low under such conditions and the slit trenches and breast-works saved countless lives. But the bombardment was far from wasteful. It had been Yamashita's deliberate policy to pour down such a withering attack that communications would be completely disrupted. Line communications were cut in many cases every 10 metres, cutting off the isolated pockets of defenders from their headquarters and more importantly, preventing any contact between headquarters and the artillery and searchlights. The fire was so intense that it was impossible to carry out any repairs to the lines.

Radios would have been invaluable but they had been sent in for repairs when the brigade got back to the island and by the 7th they had still not been returned. They finally arrived on the morning of the 8th but by then it was too late for them to be used effectively.

A heavy air raid was launched on Gordon Bennett's headquarters outside Bukit Timah and then as soon as the aircraft had departed, the artillery took over. Casualties were kept to a minimum by slit trenches and shelters, but the office truck received a direct hit and there was paper flying everywhere. Bennett noted with satisfaction in his diary that 'a little less paper in this war will improve matters'.

It seemed impossible, but as dusk fell the shelling became even more intense until now it was impossible to separate the individual explosions. There was just one endless, terrifying, deafening noise. But in spite of its ferocity, neither Bennett nor Percival believed that it was the signal that the assault was about to begin; they interpreted it as a softening up bombardment, but one that would last for several days, destroying communications and intimidating their men. And Percival was still not conceding that it was looking increasingly certain that the landing would take place on the north-west. The 18th Division was under attack, but with nothing like the ferocity in the north-west.

Shortly after 8.30 that evening the artillery fire on the Australian positions suddenly lifted and the shells were passing harmlessly over their heads to fall further inland. At that moment every man knew that the Japanese were coming.

Bennett had retired to bed early but concerned at the level of fire on the 22nd Brigade, he had got up and telephoned his duty officer, Major Dawkins, telling him to ask 22nd's headquarters if there had been any reports from the forward posts. Brigade Headquarters was also situated some distance back from the front. They replied that all the lines to the forward posts had been cut but that linesmen were endeavouring to repair them. As Dawkins appeared to be unworried, Bennett went back to bed.

But his uneasiness did not leave him and at about 11.00 p.m. he told his ADC to drive him to his operations room. He was still there at 11.30 when a telephone call from Taylor broke the news that the Japanese had landed and had already penetrated his positions.

It was exactly 9.30 when the first Japanese assault craft began moving down stream from their camouflaged positions towards the Johore Strait. The artillery shells and mortars screamed over the heads of the men of the Japanese 5th and 18th Divisions and the sound of the bursting shells drowned the noise of their engines as the landing craft began their hazardous crossing of the strait.

They waited tensely for the Allied searchlights to come on, the moment in the whole operation when they would be most vulnerable, but miraculously nothing happened. They had no way of knowing that Brigadier Taylor had given strict orders that the lights, which he had brought from Mersing, were not to be switched on except on his personal instructions. The break in communications with his front line meant that his order could not be passed by line and there was no back-up signal by Very light or radio. The lights stayed off.

By 10.30 the Australians could make out the first approaching landing craft, dark against the water, and then suddenly there seemed to be boats everywhere. They opened fire on them with a withering blast of machine gun and rifle fire and at first it was like shooting rats in a barrel. First one boat and then two more caught fire and floated across the water burning fiercely and lighting it up so that for a moment it looked like a splendid water pageant. In the light of the flames, the defenders with a view across the water could see the enormity of the force that was coming against them.

As one boat was sunk or beaten off, a dozen more took its place and the Japanese came in relentlessly, swamping the Australians with their sheer weight of numbers. The Australians waited impatiently for the pre-arranged killing area, the shore and the strait itself, to be brilliantly illuminated. This was the very core of the plan for beating off the Japanese and the Allies' only hope of catching them when they were vulnerable.

Instead the only light came from the burning boats and the

Australians cursed and shouted as they stumbled against each other and peered into the darkness looking for a target that they could shoot at.

There should have been a barrage of fire from their own artillery, but again there was nothing for the batteries too were waiting for orders down the shattered lines. When flares were fired in the agreed alternative signal, the batteries mistook them for Japanese flares.

At last the artillery in the 44th Indian Brigade's area to the south started firing, including the big 6-inch guns at Pasir Laba, but the poor visibility and lack of observation made their fire wild and inaccurate. Some of the shells began falling on the Australians' own lines so that they found themselves with an enemy in front of them and their own people bombarding them from the rear. With some difficulty the firing was stopped.

There was hand-to-hand fighting as the Japanese shot and bayoneted their way through the 22nd Brigade's positions. But if it was fierce, it hardly justified the ecstatic language of the Japanese Army Information Service in its report of the fighting: 'The courageous warriors of our landing forces... gradually closed in on the enemy position through the concentrated fire of machine guns and mortars. Words cannot describe the glorious hand grenade and hand-to-hand fighting encountered in various places by these courageous warriors after destroying layer after layer of barbed wire entanglements.'

In the assault the 2/20th lost its commanding officer, second-in-command and three company commanders and not one man who was seen wounded but alive, but who could not be brought out safely, was heard of again. The Commanding Officer, Lieutenant-Colonel C. F. Assheton, a civil engineer before the war, was wounded in the assault and a rescue party went through heavy fire to bring him in. But Assheton ordered them back from what would have been a suicidal mission. The belief in the battalion is that he then shot himself to avoid being taken alive by the Japanese.

There was now absolute confusion in the Allied lines as the Japanese swept through them and then turned to attack them from the rear. The Australians had no compasses and once they lost sight of the strait and were in the dark, featureless jungle, they did not even know what direction they were facing.

Their orders were that if they were overwhelmed by the

Japanese, the survivors were to fight their way back to Company Headquarters or as a last resort battalions were to form perimeters around their own headquarters and endeavour to make a stand.

That night 13 000 Japanese troops landed and fell against just two Australian battalions; at dawn they would be followed by another 10 000. From the Sultan's palace in Johore Bahru, Yamashita saw the coloured signal flares that he was waiting for and knew that the landings had been accomplished satisfactorily.

By midnight the Japanese were ashore in force, causing panic and chaos. Bennett sent his solitary reserve battalion forward to Taylor and ordered him to counter-attack at dawn while the Japanese were reorganising, but the Japanese anticipated him and instead attacked Taylor's own position at first light, infiltrating his lines and causing many more casualties.

By 1.00 a.m. all three battalions were already falling back, trying frantically to organise some kind of defensive position further inland. But communications were all but non-existent and in the darkness and the jungle it was every man for himself. Men became separated and missed their assembly areas so that they kept stumbling on in the dark with no notion of where they were heading.

Some had dropped their packs and weapons and were wearing only shorts, while others had no boots on and a few did not even have trousers. All were covered with mud from head to foot, scratched and bleeding, exhausted and beaten, as one eye-witness remembers the headlong flight away from the Japanese.

The men who suffered most were the young soldiers who had been enlisted and hurriedly put on a ship for Singapore. They included those who arrived never having fired a rifle or seen a bren gun and now they paid dearly for their inexperience. In an emergency they did not know how to save themselves and many died — most died — where more experienced men would have reacted faster and had at least a chance of surviving.

As the survivors of 2/20th pulled back, they imagined they could hear the Japanese all around them, but they could never see anything to fire at. They spent the remainder of the night somewhere near the Tengah airfield clustered together in a small group, deliberating on just how any operation could go quite so disastrously wrong.

At first light they met other units of the brigade also on the move, withdrawing in what they hoped was the direction of their prepared positions. The men of 2/20th moved off in extended line, passing through what a few hours before had been B-Echelon lines. The Japanese had been there before them. Tents were upturned and several bodies lay sprawled around the site, both Australian and Japanese.

They were attacked by sniper fire, but after all they had been through, it hardly bothered them and they made no attempt to track its source down but hurried on. They crossed a dirt road and were in a wide paddock lined on either side with trees. They had just got down in the long grass and were bunching up when a woodpecker machine gun opened up on them from the far end of the field.

Someone went off in a flanking movement and killed the two men on the machine gun. The Platoon Commander suddenly began shooting wildly up into the trees where he said he could see snipers. Nobody fell out of the trees so they told him his imagination had gone to pot and hurried on. Suddenly they came out on to the bank of the Kranji River and found themselves trapped, with the water ahead of them and the Japanese behind.

The Kranji at that point was still tidal and the river was about 60 m wide and too deep to be waded. Many of the Australians could not swim and many more were injured and it was only the chance discovery of two canoes that saved them. Two men in particular, Bernie Bluhdhorn and George Hartley, saw the Australians safely across. In groups of six they ferried them over the river, taking the wounded first and then the non-swimmers.

At one point, a canoe was in mid-stream when a Brewster Buffalo came over very low and they all cheered because they thought that at last they had air support. The Buffalo came down almost to the water level and only then did they see that it was wearing not the red, white and blue of the Allied air forces, but the Rising Sun of Japan. It must have been captured on the mainland. The six men in the canoe panicked, tipped over and were all drowned without the Buffalo firing a shot.

Three bren-gunners were put in a small semi-circle to keep away any Japanese who came too close and when the last of the non-swimmers was safely across, these men on the machine-guns were called in. Frank Hole, on the gun nearest the water, got no reply from the others when he called and when he went closer he saw that both were dead, probably shot by a Japanese sniper.

As the last of the Australians came out of the water on the far side, they made for a road which they could see in the distance. Just as they reached it, they were stopped in their tracks by what had to be a mirage. Getting out of a car and coming towards them was a British brigadier in full service dress with scarlet cap-band and epaulettes; and beside him on the end of a lead were two immaculately groomed bulldogs. The brigadier asked if they could tell him what was happening and then he thanked them politely, got back in the car and drove off towards the battle front.

In a much larger group now, for many other stragglers had caught up with them at the river, they set off once more in what they hoped was the direction of Singapore town. Late that afternoon after getting a lift in a truck for the last kilometre, they arrived back at their Brigade Headquarters outside Bukit Timah. They reported to the General Base Depot in Bukit Timah and for the first time in weeks, with the Japanese breathing down their necks, they slept in real beds with real pillows.

A Humiliating Surrender

While the 22nd Brigade had been taking the full force of the Japanese assault, Brigadier Maxwell's 27th Brigade to their right on the other side of the Kranji had not been vigorously attacked at all. As dawn broke on the 9th, after a night in which few of them had slept, they wondered how much longer their reprieve would last. By the time the sun was over the horizon, they had their answer for the Japanese artillery was already pounding them mercilessly and enemy fighter-bombers screamed overhead pouring bombs down on them.

Maxwell was concerned by the gaping hole in his left flank since the 22nd Brigade's departure during the night. He had no way of knowing just what had happened, but he did know that he was now vulnerable on every side.

A signal arrived advising him that Brigadier Taylor was to hold a position on the Jurong 'switch' line and that his own battalion commanders must be ready to withdraw to join the northern end of the line; yet they also had the task of holding their position against any further Japanese landing forces who came over the strait. Most of their forward telephone lines were quickly cut, as they had been with the 22nd, and communication became difficult or non-existent.

The barrage went on all day, with almost the same ferocity as the bombardment of the 22nd, until at 8.30 that evening it suddenly stopped and there was an eerie silence. This time a few of the Australian searchlights were switched on to reveal many Japanese landing craft, almost defenceless, in the middle of the strait. Jubilantly the defenders called urgently for artillery fire to blast the assault craft out of the water, but for the second consecutive day, nothing happened. The line had been shattered and when they fired their flares in the pre-arranged signal, the gunners again did not recognise them.

The Imperial Guards Division had watched impatiently as the 5th and 18th Divisions had set off the previous night on their mission. As the elite unit of the Japanese army, they had wanted to be the first ashore on Singapore, but Yamashita believed they were still battle-weary and he made them wait until the second wave. At dawn, however, they knew that the infantry had been successful and they heard the artillery barrage open up on the 27th Brigade to start the softening up process that would end with their own landing on the island.

When the searchlights came on they were momentarily dazzled, but they quickly shot out the lights and tensed themselves for the artillery attack that had to follow. To their amazement, nothing happened. In the darkness, however, and with the tide coming in, many of their boats began to drift off course and ended up in swamps or along some of the numerous creeks that emptied into the strait. Many of their men were trapped in the swamps by the rising tide and were caught in the cross-fire.

As before, though, they had such an advantage in numbers that once they began to pour ashore, the Australians were powerless to hold them. Again there was fighting at close quarters, hand-to-hand, with many dying on both sides. But by midnight the Japanese had forced Maxwell's left-hand battalion, the 2/26th, well back from the coast. The 2/30th, guarding the causeway and with its flanks bare and threatened, also withdrew.

Maxwell had been told to delay his withdrawal long enough for several oil tanks in his area to be destroyed, but this took longer than planned when the demolition truck sent to do the job received a direct hit from a shell. The demolition officer survived and instead of blowing the installation up, he opened the valves and let the oil run out into Johore Strait before going back for more explosives. Then he set it alight.

It had been the dread of the Japanese that Percival would do this and as the burning oil floated back into the swamps and streams where it caught many of their landing craft and cremated the men in them, they assumed that it was a deliberate plan to turn the whole strait into a carpet of fire. One battalion was safely ashore when the fire was started and the remainder of the Guards Division was waiting to cross. Their commanding officer made an urgent plea to Yamashita to be allowed to call off the rest of the attack that night and make their landing the next morning on the same beach-head that had been established the night before.

Before replying Yamashita sent three officers across to Singapore Island to investigate and by the time they reached the front, most of the flames had died down. There was no longer any reason to hold back. At about 4.30 a.m. on 10 February, the Guards completed their landing. Some of the atrocities which they committed later — though hardly the ones they had carried out already — were claimed to be revenge for the burning of their colleagues.

By the time the remainder of the Guards Division was ashore, the 27th Brigade was 3 km back from the coast on the slopes of the Bukit Mandai hills and the Japanese moved quickly to subdue the western flank of Heath's Northern Area.

Bennett's primary concern now was to hold and reinforce the Kranji-Jurong Line which was all that stood between the Japanese 5th and 18th Divisions and an easy drive into Singapore itself. The Imperial Guards Division was heading to seize the eastern half of the island.

There was confused and often very brave fighting on the Jurong Line which included some of the fiercest exchanges that occurred on the island. There was no longer even the pretence of air support, for the last British or Australian aircraft had been seen on the 9th. The remnants of a squadron of Hurricanes, which had fought bravely and against impossible odds, was then withdrawn to the Dutch East Indies.

Bad communications continued to dog Bennett's resistance and one of the most serious misunderstandings arose when Brigadier Taylor, perhaps suffering from many nights without sleep, misunderstood an order and withdrew part of his brigade too far at a critical moment in the battle. Shortly afterwards the men of the 44th Indian Brigade noticed one of its battalions moving its position and believed, or chose to believe, that it was a general retreat. The whole brigade fell back in disarray for 7 km.

There were many wasteful incidents when command seems to

have broken down altogether. An Australian unit known as 'X' Battalion was formed from the remnants of 22nd Brigade who had made their way to Singapore and it had a strength of about 200 men. They were a scratch force, poorly armed — some had only hand grenades while others had no weapons at all and carried only ammunition — and with no clear-cut battalion loyalty.

A former member of 'X' Battalion remembers that 'they just rounded up any spare troops they could find in the depot, called us out on parade and said that from now on we were X Battalion'. They were given a rather vague mission that would take them close to or even behind the Japanese lines near Bukit Timah. At about mid-day they were driven some distance up the Bukit Timah Road and then told to keep marching until they came to a cross-roads where they would make contact with some Punjabis.

British troops whom they passed going in the other direction — the sensible direction, they agreed — told them lurid stories of the Japanese just ahead and all around them they could see buildings smouldering or on fire. They were fired on several times by snipers, but kept marching along the road as they had been told. They never did find the Punjabis and they sensed that if they went much further the only people they would make contact with would be Japanese.

Three men were sent ahead on patrol but they never returned (they were caught by the Japanese, held for twenty-four hours and then executed), and suddenly their pointless route march was becoming much more dangerous.

They turned off the road on to a track, still looking for the Punjabis, or by now for any other Australians or Allies. After two kilometres the track led them through country that was a tangle of bog and thicket, so thick that they had to hold on to each other's bayonet scabbards to maintain contact. At last as darkness was falling, they called a halt when they found themselves out on the side of a hill. They were so tired that as soon as their heads touched the ground, they fell asleep.

The next thing they knew, all hell had broken loose. The Japanese, in a well-orchestrated attack, had overpowered the sentries before they could give the alarm and had got right into the middle of them. They had sent up a flare so that it was as bright as daylight and from the top of the hill they were rolling grenades down on to them and screaming and laughing. The only thing that saved the Australians was that the Japanese were using inefficient concussion-type grenades which were much less effective than the deadly shrapnel Mills bombs which were standard issue for the Australians.

As they stumbled sleepily to their feet or tried to roll clear, the flare mercifully went out but some were too slow to escape. The Japanese with bayonets fixed rushed down the hill at them yelling wildly. A woodpecker machine gun, its rate of fire slow and deliberate compared with the rapid fire of the brens, began firing on them from the bottom of the paddock and they could see the flame from the barrel, but not the gun itself or the man behind it.

Someone threw a grenade and the machine gun went silent and the next moment the Australians were over the side of the hill and running through what seemed to be Chinese gardens as fast as their legs would carry them. There was the sound of firing all around them, but it didn't seem to be aimed particularly at them until they suddenly ran into a barrage of mortar bombs which the Japanese were hurling at a defended position that seemed to have been abandoned.

Bren-gunner Frank Hole, his gun still strapped to his back, dived for the nearest hole and found himself falling down and down. He had jumped into a native well and the wall was so slimy that when he tried to break his fall, he couldn't get a grip. Eventually he managed to stop, about 4 m below the ground, by wedging himself from wall to wall. It smelled dank and horrible.

He tried to climb out but the walls were so slippery that he couldn't move and the weight of the bren threatened to send him plummeting down into the blackness below him. It suddenly struck him as funny that after surviving all the horrors of the war, he was going to die unnoticed at the bottom of a stinking well and he laughed out loud. He wondered how long it would be before the owner of the well noticed that his water was polluted.

One of his mates, though, had seen the whole performance and had watched in admiration as Hole, nearly 200 cm tall, had leaped like Superman straight over the side of the well and disappeared down the hole. By leaning down as far as he could and then holding out his rifle, he could just get it into Hole's hand and he felt a firm grip being taken. It took nearly twenty minutes to get him out but at last he scrambled over the edge and lay gasping like a fish on the ground, oblivious of the mortar shells bursting all around him.

It had been one o'clock when they had awoken to find the Japanese rolling grenades down on them. Though it seemed like an eternity, only ten minutes had passed when Frank Hole went down the well. They came out of the gardens into a big paddock where the ground was more swampy, but with tall grass and trees round the edge that gave some cover from view. They got down in a semi-circle for better protection and decided to stay there until daylight.

In the darkness they had not realised that they were very close to the track and at about four in the morning those who were asleep were woken by what sounded like a big crowd of people running. It took only a few moments for them to realise that it *was* a big crowd of people running and they were awake instantly, all of them that is except one corporal from 'B' Company who grunted and turned over.

The footsteps came closer and the Australians sank lower into the grass and then suddenly the runners were almost on top of them, 600 tough-looking Japanese troops going past at a jog trot. They had just drawn level when the corporal began to snore, not a gentle snore that might have gone undetected, but a full throated rattle that would have stopped a man at a hundred paces.

The others didn't know what to do. They didn't dare wake him in case he shouted out in English, but they were so close to the Japanese that if they had reached out they could have touched their ankles. For once luck was with them and the Japanese, breathing heavily from their exertion, apparently heard nothing. As the last of them jogged past, the Australians studied each other's expressions in the moonlight that was filtering through the grass and for the first time that night they felt almost cheerful. They kicked the corporal and felt better.

They eventually made their way back to Singapore, which they calculated was now about a three-hour march away, and ended the whole pointless and tragic exercise in the back of an old planter's truck which deposited them outside the Union Jack Club across the road from the glittering cathedral of St Andrews.

Conditions in Singapore were chaotic. Although the artillery fire was only sporadic, there were Chinese and Malays running in every direction. Mingling with them were the British, Australian and Indian stragglers and deserters looking mainly for loot and a chance to get off the island. Many of them, by the fairness of their skin, seemed to be recent arrivals.

An Australian naval officer who was in Singapore on special duties at the time with the Royal Navy remembers the lack of troop discipline, the widespread looting and the general air of defeatism as one of the blackest parts of the campaign. 'And the Australians were always the worst,' he recalls. 'The best when they were good, the worst when they were bad.'

There were other more inexplicable incidents which this same officer, whose work made him admirably suited to see at first hand what was going on, remembers with shame. 'There was one group of Australians that had been getting a terrible pasting and the Japanese were coming across every day and machine-gunning them from the air. One day they just threw down their weapons and said they weren't going to fight any more.

'There were two or three officers there at the time and the senior of them was almost pleading with them not to lay down their arms, but to no avail. I reported what had happened, but I think the whole thing was hushed up afterwards.'

It was at about this time that Brigadier Taylor, who was on no better terms with Bennett than he had been before the hostilities started, reached the end of his tether and was replaced. A few men from 'X' Battalion were standing around outside Brigade Headquarters just before it moved from Bukit Timah to Holland Road in the city. They watched Taylor walking away from them along the road and saw him suddenly crumple up and lurch forwards. He was immediately helped to his feet by a young officer but they could see that he was catching his breath and hunched over as though in pain.

Only that morning a warning had been issued that Japanese snipers were causing more trouble than usual and their first thought was that he had been shot by one of them although they had heard nothing. They saw Taylor being put into a car and taken off at high speed but it was not until much later that they learned that he had not been shot, but had collapsed from sheer exhaustion. In his concern for his men and his duty he had not slept since the landing.

Major Charles Moses who in civilian life had been General Manager of the Australian Broadcasting Commission and was now on Bennett's staff made a remarkable bid for safety when he was trapped by the Japanese on the Jurong Road outside the city. He described later how he crept up to his car and starting it as silently as he could, sped away in the direction of Singapore.

140

He heard yelling and suddenly there were 'dark, solid objects' across his path and in the headlights he saw what were unmistakeably scores of Japanese soldiers. The solid objects turned out to be tanks and no sooner had he recognised them than someone opened fire from a range of less than 5 m with a machine gun, smashing the car's radiator. Moses flung open the door and running fast doubled back up the street pursued by Japanese fire. The next moment the tanks started firing into the car reducing it to a heap of metal.

His army boots clattering on the road, Moses covered the last 200 m at a speed he wouldn't have thought possible. When he had passed the last house in the village he crossed a small stream and scrambled up a bank on the other side and on up a hill into a *lalang* where he collapsed exhausted and got his breath back.

He heard shouting from the village, some of it in English, and knew that he must move on at once. Branches crackled under his feet and scratched against his helmet and immediately a voice called out nearby in Japanese. He froze then very carefully took off his boots and helmet and laid them under a tree, moving forward silently in stockinged feet. A dog came out of a house and snapped at his heels, but got bored and left him.

Three hours later he still seemed to be as far from safety as ever and he was beginning to despair. Then his luck changed and he came out into a Chinese cemetery and shortly afterwards found himself on the Bukit Timah Road. Troops were pulling back and Moses tried to get them to move over to the other side of the railway embankment where they could mount an ambush on the Japanese who must have been very close behind. They refused and in the end Moses had to threaten to shoot the British officer who was leading them before he would obey him.

Most people found the sheer size of Moses daunting enough. Before the war he had played Rugby Union for Victoria and he had been the State's amateur heavyweight boxing champion.

By the night of the 10th, the Bukit Timah hill was in the hands of the Japanese and the Rising Sun flew above it. From the summit there was a commanding view over the city and Yamashita had already decided that when he had possession of the hill, he would call on Percival to surrender. Early on the morning of the 11th he sent a solitary reconnaissance plane to fly low over Singapore and drop twenty-nine copies of a demand for surrender, written in

English and Japanese, and addressed to 'The High Command of the British Army'.

There was a special significance to 11 February which had not escaped V. G. Bowden, the Australian Government's representative in Singapore. He had cabled only two days earlier that 'It appears significant that February 11th is greatest Japanese patriotic festival of the year, namely anniversary of accession of their first Emperor and it can be taken as certain that they will make a supreme effort to achieve capture of Singapore on this date.'

Each copy of the surrender demand was rolled in a wooden tube 45 cm long, with red and white streamers at the end to make it more visible. The rather elaborate wording had been compiled by Yamashita's English-speaking intelligence officer, Lieutenant-Colonel Ichiji Sugita. On the face of it, it was a courteous and considerate offer to cease hostilities that did not rule out terms that would modify the humiliation of surrender.

Your Excellency,

I, the High Command of the Nippon Army based on the spirit of Japanese chivalry, have the honour of presenting this note to Your Excellency advising you to surrender the whole force in Malaya.

My sincerest respect is due to your army which true to the traditional spirit of Great Britain, is bravely defending Singapore which now stands isolated and unaided. Many fierce and gallant fights have been fought by your gallant men and officers, to the honour of British warriorship. But the developments of the general war situation has already sealed the fate of Singapore, and the continuation of futile resistance would only serve to inflict direct harm and injuries to thousands of non-combatants living in the city, throwing them into further miseries and horrors of war, but also would not add anything to the honour of your army.

I expect that Your Excellency accepting my advice will give up this meaningless and desperate resistance and promptly order the entire front to cease hostilities and will despatch at the same time your parliamentaire [delegation] according to the procedure shown at the end of this note. If on the contrary, Your Excellency should neglect my advice and the present resistance be continued, I shall be obliged, though reluctantly from humanitarian considerations to order my army to make annihilating attacks on Singapore.

In closing this note of advice, I pay again my sincere respects to Your Excellency.

(signed) Tomoyuki Yamashita

1. The Parliamentaire shall proceed to the Bukit Timah Road.
2. The Parliamentaire should bear a large white flag and the Union Jack.

Yamashita had hardly overstated the desperate situation. The Japanese had entered Bukit Timah village and the base at about the same time the surrender demands were being dropped on the city and they now had all the fuel, food and supply dumps so that Percival suddenly found himself with barely two weeks' food left and almost no petrol.

The reservoir area was in danger of falling into Japanese hands whenever they chose so that he could no longer even guarantee a water supply to the city and the danger of an epidemic breaking out would be so high that it could decimate the population without another shot being fired.

The constant air raids had already smashed many of the water mains, reducing pressure to a trickle and allowing the precious water to run to waste in the drains.

Percival had no authority to surrender even if his inclinations had been to do so. He had no orders countermanding Churchill's instruction to Wavell that there was to be 'no thought of sparing the troops or sparing the population' and that all commanders and senior officers were expected to die with their troops. He therefore ignored the message and cabled Wavell that he did not intend to reply.

Instead he ordered Maxwell's 27th Brigade to recapture Bukit Panjang village to the north of Bukit Timah as the first step of an effort to recapture Bukit Timah itself. It was a foolhardy idea from the start and the combination of poor communications and a fierce attack by the Imperial Guards so undermined the Australians that instead of attacking Bukit Panjang the brigade found itself split in two, with one battalion below the Bukit Timah Road and one right up by the Pierce Reservoir. After a fierce engagement, the survivors limped back to Singapore.

Over in the east of the island there was fierce fighting. A battle raged outside the gates of Changi prison for three days. There were no guards left in the gaol and at about 5.00 in the evening on 12 February, a group of convicts broke into the prison armoury and stole rifles and pistols, as a prelude to starting a riot.

Among the 700 prisoners were 30 Japanese, all but one of whom had been detained as enemy aliens. Within hours of the landings at Kota Bharu, most of the Japanese community who had not already made their escape, were arrested and held in Changi and later transferred to India. These were either too old or sick to make the journey or had been arrested after the transfer to India.

The odd man out was a former consular official, Mamoru Shinozaki, who was serving six months for espionage. Shinozaki, who was afterwards singled out by thousands of Europeans and Chinese, including the Governor's wife, for his humanity during the occupation, played on the fact that he was a Japanese officer and therefore an enemy of the British administration which had put them behind bars. He ordered the rioters to lay down their weapons in a heap at his feet. To his astonishment, they obeyed him.

Shinozaki reasoned that the inside of the gaol was probably about the safest place on the island, barring a direct hit from artillery or bombers, which he thought unlikely. The Allies and the Japanese both knew that the prison contained their own people.

To ensure that they would remain undisturbed, he securely locked the main gates on the inside and some old Japanese women detainees made a Japanese flag out of a bed-sheet with the rising sun painted in red ink, which he hung outside the main gate of the gaol.

There was a clock tower at the front of the prison and the Japanese spent hours up there with a bird's eye view of the fighting, trying to guess which way the battle was swinging. They noticed that the Japanese gun-fire always seemed to be green, while the answering fire from the Allies was yellow. Some of the Japanese were helping Shinozaki take the looted weapons back to the armoury when the top of the tower, miraculously empty at the time, scored a direct hit from an artillery shell.

Unperturbed they put out the fire and went back to watch the battle. They could see that nearby Selarang Barracks, occupied by

Allied troops, was on fire and that there was a large group of Australian soldiers outside the prison gates who seemed undecided where to go next. The Australians tried in vain to open the prison gates and then moved off.

Shinozaki was concerned most about how he was going to keep order in the prison. The convicts who had laid down the guns were becoming increasingly restless and some of them were desperate criminals. He doubted if he could get them to obey him twice. When he came down from the tower after watching Selarang ablaze, he found some of them already looting the stores and he decided to resolve the problem once and for all.

He shouted, 'Hi! Anyone want to get out? I'll get you out of gaol!' And they were round him in a rush, some with their looted goods already packed and on their shoulders. He told them that from now on they were on their own; that once they were outside the gates, they could not return but would have to take their chance.

About five hundred of the convicts, many serving long sentences for murder, robbery and crimes of violence, streamed through the gates, leaving behind two hundred whom Shinozaki organised into teams for cooking, medical care, guard duties and so on. The old and the women were put into the prison hospital.

Outside, the fighting gradually moved away from Changi and the battle for Singapore continued as the Japanese got closer to the city and the harbour. Many of the convicts who were released went straight to settle old scores, particularly against the police, before losing themselves in the anonymity and chaos of the city.

Two days before Yamashita had issued his ultimatum, Percival had seen that it was now only a question of time before the Japanese had control of Bukit Timah Road and that once they were on it, they would have a clear run into the city.

Early on the 10th he had issued his plan for withdrawing all his troops inside a huge perimeter that would stretch round the city itself. A withdrawal to the eastern end of the island and to Changi which had been an option was now ruled out for the whole area was in the control of the Imperial Guards. Inside the area that he had designated were the main supply areas and hospitals, two of the three reservoirs, Kallang Airfield and Bukit Timah. All this had changed within twenty-four hours and he no longer had the reservoirs or Bukit Timah.

By the 12th, Yamashita knew that his note was being ignored and he stepped up the tempo of his attack. There was now no point in Percival maintaining forces in the Northern or Eastern Areas and the Western Area had long since fallen. It was clearly time to fall back into the final perimeter which had already been substantially reduced by the speed of the Japanese advance.

On that day, Thursday the 12th, he gave the order that the perimeter was to be established that night and General Heath began pulling back his 11th Indian Division and what was left of the 18th at noon. They were harassed all the way by the Japanese, communications were all but non-existent and few of the military commanders, let alone the troops, had a clear picture of what was going on. V. G. Bowden was close to the mark when he observed, 'Except as a fortress and battlefield, Singapore has ceased to exist.'

Friday the 13th saw the fiercest and most intense gunfire of any day since the Japanese landed. It didn't seem possible but the Japanese seemed to have found yet more guns and more ammunition. It was an extraordinary, fearful experience for military and civilians alike as shells arrived at intervals of only one or two seconds for hours on end while machine gun and rifle fire criss-crossed the city from every direction. If Yamashita was trying to wage a war of attrition it was clear that he would succeed for no city could survive for long under such a bombardment.

Most of the troops were exhausted and many of the British and Indians, who felt as though they had been retreating without a break since Kota Bharu, wanted to do nothing but sleep. Some just took off their boots and ignoring the bedlam all around them, closed their eyes and slept.

Many of them went into the old building of Robinson's store and lay down on the bare floor for a few minutes sleep. They were still there, Australians, British and Indians, when Japanese bombers came over and blasted the building. The bombers seemed to be looking for the building because they flew around for a few minutes as though wanting to be sure that they had pinpointed the right target. More than a hundred bodies were dug out of the wreckage.

At the 10th Australian Base Hospital near Bukit Timah the treatment of the wounded had gone on ceaselessly, day and night, and the medical staff hardly noticed the war waging outside the school walls unless a bomb or shell came too close. Then on the evening of the 10th, they were suddenly aware of firing just outside the building and bullets began to hit the walls all around them.

Hardly pausing, they grabbed the wounded, threw them on to a truck and raced into the city. They went straight to Singapore General Hospital where the doctors believed they could most safely finish the surgery they had been performing. Here they saw a sight that none of them would ever forget.

The Singapore Hospital had enormously long corridors and there, lying mutilated on the floor, was a line of men, women and children stretching as far as the eye could see, crawling or dragging themselves along, or being helped by orderlies, all waiting their turn to reach the operating theatre.

'I thought that going to war was going to be a great personal experience, a refining in fire,' a surgeon with the AIF in Singapore recalls, 'but it wasn't a great refining, it was awful. Just bloody, bloody awful.'

The following day the Indian Base Hospital caught fire. It spread so fast through the wooden huts that in spite of very brave rescue attempts by men of the Argylls and Gordons, most of the patients perished.

On the 13th the Japanese engineers finally succeeded in repairing the causeway and the heavy artillery and the remaining XXV Army tanks which had not been ferried across poured over to support the last Japanese offensive.

There were pockets of very heavy fighting that day, particularly involving the 1st Malayan Brigade which was in position on the south coast just west of the city, as well as on Pasir Penjang Ridge and astride Ayer Rajah Road immediately to the north of the ridge. This Malayan Brigade was fighting with four battalions, two with British troops and two with Malayans.

The Japanese at last forced their way through. This push brought the British Military Hospital at Alexandra within their control. The hospital staff attempted to surrender, but the Japanese ignored them and instead ran amok, bayonetting doctors and patients including one on the operating table. The survivors were then herded into small rooms without food or water and in the morning were killed.

That morning, too, on Friday the 13th, Rear-Admiral E. J. Spooner, who was in charge of all naval establishments on Singapore, had reached the decision that he would take his remaining ships and any other sea-going craft in Singapore across to Java. There was accommodation on these for about 3000 people as well as the crews. Spooner told Percival that this would certainly be the last opportunity for any organised evacuation from the island. Even then it could be a hazardous journey.

At a conference later that day, Percival said that 1800 of these berths had been allotted to the military forces on the island and that 100 of these could be taken up by Australians. The choice of who was to go was left to Bennett and he decided that only those whose expertise in some field would help the ultimate war effort should be evacuated. The group he selected included a strong contingent of signals officers and men.

Many might have done better to take their chance on Singapore. Of the hundred whom Bennett chose, only thirty-nine eventually reached safety after being attacked by the Japanese. Both Admiral Spooner and Air Vice-Marshal Pulford, the Air Officer Commanding Far East, were among those who perished.

On Percival's orders the last of the Australian nursing sisters and the two matrons of the Australian General Hospitals, who had been hurriedly taken away from their wards, were ordered on board the British steamship *Vyner Brooke* for the journey back to Australia. It had been decided not to tell them that their hurried evacuation, which they resented bitterly as long as there were patients for them to care for, was because of grave fears that the Japanese would massacre any nursing staff they found, as they had in Hong Kong. The murders at Alexandra had not yet been revealed.

The *Vyner Brooke* left at once and had steamed for two days before Japanese Naval Air Force aircraft bombed and sank it as it was passing down the east coast of Sumatra. Several of the nurses and the two matrons managed to get ashore on Banka Island where the Japanese murdered every one of them except one sister, Vivian Bullwinkel, who feigned death and survived her wounds.

The Australian Government's representative, V. G. Bowden, had advised his government that Singapore could not be held with the existing forces and that its fall was imminent. He asked whether he and his Political and Commercial Secretaries should stay, or leave on a cargo vessel while there was still a chance. The Australian War Cabinet replied that they should remain in Singapore and it expressed its deep appreciation of what Bowden had done.

The following day, however, Cabinet had a change of mind and in a second cable told Bowden that if the situation got too dangerous, he was to 'insist on receiving full diplomatic privileges and courtesies' and that if necessary he was to show a paraphrase of that cable to the Japanese Administration.

On 14 February, Bowden could see that the capitulation could occur at any moment and in spite of Cabinet's instructions, he accepted an offer from a member of Percival's staff to escape with a group of senior officers and civil servants in the launch *Osprey*. Bowden and his secretaries embarked and *Osprey* took them out to a larger vessel, the *Mary-Rose* which sailed at once. But the Japanese attacked her too and she was captured in Banka Strait. When Bowden demanded an interview with a Japanese officer to disclose his diplomatic status, he was murdered.

The area allocated to General Bennett in the last perimeter was in a pleasant suburb which had some of Singapore's finest old houses, many of them with extensive gardens and tennis courts, some with their larders and wine cellars stocked as though for a siege. All the houses had been abandoned and his men dug in.

On his own initiative Bennett had decided to form a perimeter with his AIF units and to make his final stand in this position which was about 8 km from the city centre. He now had all the Australians on the island with him except for those in hospital as well as a company of 2nd Gordon Highlanders. Even the Australian stragglers had been rounded up and sent to him.

He put his men in an all-round defensive position to meet any Japanese force that tried to break through and take them from the rear and there, he told them, they would make their final stand. Even without further supplies, there was enough food and water for ten days.

The Australians had seen the order that they were to stand firm and if necessary die where they were and they were content enough with that. Their morale was high. They mistook what they saw as a successful local attempt to repulse a small unit of Japanese as meaning that they were at least evenly matched with them. They had no way of knowing how the battle was going elsewhere on the island and Bennett did not tell them.

Some of the men of 2/20th went on a reconnaissance of the house whose garden they were occupying near the tennis court. They found very little food in the house, but whoever had lived there had assembled a remarkable collection of pornography hidden in a camphor-wood chest. The words were in Dutch or German but the pictures needed no translation.

In other deserted mansions all around them they found stocked larders and took steps, Bennett noted with approval, 'to see that these should not fall into the hands of the Japanese'. Not far away, the 2/30th found itself near the French Consul's house, whose cellar was stocked with splendid wine. Australian author Stan Arneil recalls how they drank the finest of the consul's wines 'by the tin pannikin'.

The Australians saw no civilians or Japanese and indeed compared with many other units on Singapore Island that day they were not under such intense bombardment or attack. The Japanese had made two unsuccessful attempts to break through their perimeter, which had heartened the AIF still further. They seemed content to leave them alone apart from blasting them periodically with mortar and artillery fire.

Within his perimeter Bennett had about 4500 men and there were another 3000 sick or wounded in hospital. Perhaps because of his concern for his men, perhaps because he no longer trusted Percival to make rational decisions, he chose that day to make one of his most extraordinary decisions. Without telling Percival, his commanding officer, he telegraphed the Australian government and told them that in certain circumstances he intended to surrender the Australians to the Japanese, even if this was in direct disobedience of Percival's and Wavell's orders.

The clear implication of this was that Percival could be fighting a last ditch battle and suddenly discover that the most important component of his army had just surrendered without telling him.

It was, as Percival generously noted when he finally learned what Bennett had done, 'a most extraordinary procedure'. It was even more extraordinary that the Australian seemed to be unable to bring himself to tell Percival what he had done.

Percival himself certainly seemed to be increasingly incapable of making urgent, on the spot decisions affecting the immediate progress of the war. One of his staff, Major Cyril Wild, wrote that during the conduct of the battle he had become used to seeing the General's 'painful inability to give a decision' and on three occasions to make any reply whatever when points of operational importance were referred to him.

Worn down by months of extreme pressure and a succession of

humiliating defeats, it may be that Percival was no longer capable of taking the calculated risks that a better and more adventurous general would have taken. This was certainly the belief of Bennett. Whether it would have made any difference to the outcome if Singapore's military forces had been commanded by, say, Montgomery is debatable; but it seems probable that he would not have gone down in history as the commander of the greatest British military disaster since Cornwallis surrendered at Yorktown.

At the meeting on the afternoon of the 13th at Percival's headquarters when the decision had been made to send out as many people as possible on the Navy's remaining ships, Heath and Bennett had argued forcefully that it was time to surrender to spare the civilians any further punishment and to protect them from being slaughtered if the Japanese suddenly broke through. Both generals thought it important that they surrender while the Japanese troops could still be controlled by their officers.

A second demand for surrender was dropped by the Japanese on the 13th, this time less polite and with a veiled threat of what might happen if the resistance continued. None of the men sitting with Percival could see any advantage in inflicting a few more casualties on the enemy or in delaying the inevitable Japanese victory by a day or two, if the price for this was the complete destruction of the Allied forces and the massacre of countless civilians.

Wavell had still not authorised Percival to surrender, however. No local commander, even of the rank of Percival, could have surrendered when his orders were to fight on without risking a charge of insubordination at best or treason at worst. Only that day Wavell had authorised last minute escapes 'by any bold and determined personnel', but had confirmed that the order was still to fight it out to the end in Singapore.

Percival agreed that a counter-attack was pointless, but he ordered them to fight on. Privately, when the others had gone, he sent Wavell a full report of the situation including the view of the other generals that they ought to surrender. He added his own belief that they could not resist for more than another day or two at the most. 'There must come a stage,' he concluded, 'when in the interests of the troops and the civil population, further bloodshed will serve no useful purpose.' But he stopped short of saying that in his personal opinion that stage had already arrived.

Percival told Wavell that he would obey his order to the last to fight on, but he asked for wider discretionary powers. Again Wavell had to refuse because Churchill had still not swerved from his original instructions.

Sir Shenton Thomas, the Governor, was also deeply disturbed by the advice that he was getting from his medical staff that a major epidemic could break out at any moment. He cabled this information to London with the request that it be treated with the greatest urgency.

That terrible black Friday at last came to an end, but the stench of death, cordite and burning hung over the city like a shroud. The furious digging in the rubble for survivors and for the dead went on ceaselessly day and night. No sane man could know what Churchill hoped to achieve by clinging to his lines of rhetoric which condemned these people to this horror.

Finally the word came from Churchill that when nothing further could be gained by fighting on, Wavell could cease resistance. 'You are of course sole judge of the moment when no further result can be gained at Singapore,' wrote the man who had said that if the Japanese ever succeeded in capturing the island, they would inherit 'only the ashes of this glittering jewel'.

Wavell immediately communicated this to Percival in a message which ended, 'Just before final cessation of fighting, opportunity should be given to any determined bodies of men or individuals to try and effect escape by any means possible. They must be armed...Whatever happens I thank you and all troops for your gallant efforts of last few days.'

Percival proposed delaying no longer and advised Wavell to that effect. He read the cable from Wavell to Heath and Bennett but for some inexplicable reason censored it and did not include the instruction about escape. Any question that it might have been left out as an oversight was discounted when Percival's book *The War in Malaya* was published and the same extract was omitted. Yet there is no question that he received the full message from Wavell because it remained on the files, and the last sentence thanking the troops was not deleted.

After attending communion Percival called a conference of his commanders for 9.30 a.m. on Sunday 15 February. This historic meeting at his underground headquarters at Fort Canning was attended by the generals and senior staff officers and except for the Commissioner of Police there were no civilians present. The decision to surrender was entirely a military one. Gordon Bennett arrived in a utility instead of his staff car because he was afraid that the car would be too tempting a target for the Japanese pilots patrolling over the city.

The atmosphere in Fort Canning, dug deep into the hill on which the old fort had been built, was grim. The Chief of Police reported that his detectives were being bombed by prisoners who had been released from Changi and that a lot of old scores were being settled. Then each of the other men around the table added to the catalogue of imminent disaster. Percival, looking tired and worried, listened to each of them in silence and the decision to surrender was unanimous.

In the surrender demands which the Japanese had dropped, they had given instructions on the procedure that Percival was to follow and Percival read them aloud again. A white flag was to be flown from the flag staff at Government House. Then a parlementaire, or delegation, would go forward through the lines carrying both a white flag and a Union Jack. In the first demand, Yamashita's headquarters had been at Bukit Timah so that the delegation would have driven up Bukit Timah Road, but now the Japanese front line was within the city limits.

Percival named the party which would carry the formal letter over his signature advising Yamashita that the Allies were willing to surrender. It consisted of three officers, Brigadier T. K. Newbeggin, his Administration Officer, Hugh Fraser, the Colonial Secretary and III Corps Staff Captain Cyril Wild who spoke Japanese. The three men left Fort Canning at 11.30 a.m. travelling in an open car with the two flags furled in the back.

They had an uncomfortable journey, making frequent detours to avoid blocked streets until they eventually reached the point where Bukit Timah Road crossed Adam and Farrer Roads, the front line of the British 54th Brigade. It was marked by a heavily mined road block.

They were viewed with curiosity and a great deal of suspicion by the British and only after convincing a patrol that they were not defecting to the Japanese were they allowed to proceed. They unfurled their flags and carrying them high, picked their way cautiously through the mine field, guided by a young officer.

Once on the other side, they had to walk an unnerving 600 m along the road, conscious of unseen weapons aimed at them on every side, before a patrol of the 5th Japanese Division intercepted them. The Japanese took away their pistols and led them into a small house beside the road where Wild tried frantically, with his limited Japanese, to explain what they were doing there and that they wanted to be taken to Yamashita's headquarters.

The Japanese treated them courteously and insisted on taking photographs of the three men with the two flags prominently displayed, but they showed little sign of doing anything else. There was a special urgency because one of the decisions taken at Fort Canning had been that the Allies would cease firing at 4.00 p.m. that afternoon and the order would already have been passed out. If nothing had been agreed with Yamashita by that time and the Japanese launched an attack, the Allies might be caught unarmed.

Another hour went by and then at last two staff officers arrived from Yamashita's headquarters. Newbeggin, who was carrying the letter from Percival outlining his proposals for a capitulation and suggesting a cease fire conference in Singapore, gave it to the senior of the two officers, a colonel.

Instead of reading it, however, the man ignored it and handed Newbeggin a typewritten letter of his own. Yamashita would not go to Singapore, they were told, but Percival would come to him at Bukit Timah at 4.30 that afternoon. The letter went on to say that the Allies must immediately cease fire, lay down their arms and remain in their positions.

As best he could, for the entire conversation was being conducted in Japanese, Wild pointed out that the Allies could hardly be expected to lay down their arms while the Japanese were still firing at them, but the colonel refused to discuss the matter. Instead he gave them a large Japanese flag which he told them was to be flown from the top of the Cathay Building as a sign that Percival had accepted the terms and was coming to meet Yamashita. With that the meeting ended.

The three men were given back their pistols and blindfolded before being driven back to a point near their front line, still clutching their flags. They negotiated the mine field, recovered their car and drove back to Fort Canning as fast as they could.

It was three o'clock when they reported back to Percival. Wild was told to take the Japanese flag at once to the Cathay Building and run it up the flag pole. The sight of it fluttering over the city brought a chill of despair to those who had endured so much to prevent this day ever happening.

The meeting between the two commanders took place at the Ford

Motor factory just above Bukit Timah. Driving in a car borrowed from the Bata Shoe Company, Percival with Newbeggin, Wild and another staff officer, were late arriving and it was 5.15 before they sat down on one side of a long table facing Yamashita and six of his senior officers. Whatever thoughts were going through the two men's minds as they looked on each other for the first time, it did not reflect in their faces. Yamashita was impatient to get on with it because it had occurred to him, when he first heard that a deputation was coming through the lines, that Percival might simply be stalling for time while reinforcements were being rushed in. He did not altogether trust the Englishman's motives in asking for a cease fire. What he knew, and Percival did not, was that the Japanese were outnumbered by three to one on the island and that the bombardment had used up so much of their ammunition and supplies that if it came to a long period of street fighting after the big guns were silenced, he would probably have been defeated.

Yamashita did not know the full extent of the devastation in the city and that food, water and ammunition were almost exhausted and that health officials were warning that an outbreak of cholera or typhoid could break out at any moment.

He was therefore anxious to end the battle as quickly as possible and he was in no mood for the long list of questions which Percival produced. He waved it aside and refused to discuss them, saying that all these details could be worked out later. All that he wanted to know immediately was whether the Allied surrender was unconditional and how soon it was to come into effect.

Percival wanted the fighting finished as much as Yamashita, but he was unwilling to sign any surrender document that did not include some guarantee of the safety of his troops and the civilians.

The discussion went backwards and forwards for what seemed an interminable time, covering the same ground over and over again. Everything had to be translated by an official interpreter who spoke very poor English, and Wild's efforts to speak Japanese only added to the confusion.

Yamashita told Percival that he had planned an attack for that evening and that if he did not hurry up and surrender, the attack would proceed. His patience was visibly becoming more strained until he angrily demanded in English that Percival answer his question.

'The time of the night attack is drawing near,' he told him

bluntly. 'Is the British Army going to surrender or not? Answer Yes or No.' And speaking in English for the first time, he emphasised the words.

Percival's time had run out and he agreed wearily to the cease fire, but asked that a thousand of his men be allowed to carry arms to maintain law and order in the city until the Japanese could take over. Yamashita agreed.

There was one more point of dissension and that was the time at which the cease fire was to come into effect. Yamashita suggested 8.30 that night, Percival wanted to wait until 10.00 to ensure that he could pass his orders to all his troops. Yamashita retorted that this was too late because it would not give him time to launch his night attack if Percival reneged. If he insisted on this time scale, then he and Sir Shenton Thomas would be held as hostages until the surrender had been completed. Once again, Percival was forced to concede and accept that the cease fire would begin at 8.30.

Almost an hour after the discussions had begun, Percival signed his name on the surrender document at 6.10 p.m. Under its terms all his troops surrendered unconditionally, all fighting would end at 8.30 that night and the Allies would remain in place and disarm themselves within an hour, with the exception of the thousand armed men who would patrol Singapore.

At the very end of the negotiations, Yamashita, increasingly impatient, had told Percival, 'You have agreed to the terms, but you have yet to make yourself clear as to whether you have agreed to an unconditional surrender or not.'

Percival, with head bowed, had nodded his agreement but Yamashita was still not satisfied. 'If you have accepted our terms,' he insisted, 'I would like to have them confirmed from your own mouth once more.'

He had repeated the conditions and added that if the Allies infringed any one of the terms, the Japanese would resume hostilities at once. Louder, Percival had said, 'I agree,' and had added one final request. 'Will the Imperial Army protect the British civilians, men, women and children?'

Yamashita had replied, 'We shall see to it. Now please sign this agreement.' There was only one copy of it and the Allies never did receive one, but for 100 000 troops the fighting was over.

When Percival left the room, Yamashita and his staff drank a victory toast in *sake* to the Emperor. On Singapore Island alone they had lost 1700 dead and 3400 injured but they had won a stunning, overwhelming victory. In only seventy days they had conquered the whole peninsula of Malaya, giving them the tin and rubber production as a bonus. The 'impregnable' fortress of Singapore, symbol of British supremacy throughout the Far East, had fallen to them in just seven days.

No amount of incompetence on the part of the Allied commanders could shake the fact that it was a magnificent victory and a humiliating defeat for the Allies. It had been meticulously planned and then executed with imagination and courage by a first-rate army. It meant far more to the Japanese than the capture of a strategically important island and its naval dockyard. The brutality of some of the Japanese troops, notably the Imperial Guards Division, was a horrible blot on what could otherwise have been a copybook campaign fought by Yamashita.

Percival, outwitted and outmanoeuvred by his counterpart, cabled Wavell for the last time, advising him that he had been unable to fight any longer. 'All ranks have done their best,' he signalled and that was more or less true. But for more than 100 000 of them who now waited meekly to be taken into captivity, it was cold comfort indeed.

Escape and Captivity

When Gordon Bennett got back to AIF Headquarters at Tanglin Barracks after the historic meeting at Fort Canning he at once called his unit commanders and told them that Percival had agreed to a surrender. Although they had all expected it, the news still came as a stunning shock.

Bennett gave orders that every man was to be re-clothed and issued with new boots, and that all ranks were to carry two days' rations in case the Japanese did not feed them. Secret papers and technical equipment were to be destroyed. A complete nominal roll was to be taken of the brigade and given to the Japanese with a request that all the names be forwarded to Australia so that the men's next of kin could know as soon as possible that they were alive and in captivity.

He then went on a last tour of his lines, taking with him his ADC and Major Charles Moses. He wanted to speak to his troops for the last time and he wanted to reconnoitre the area in some detail, for he had long ago decided that he was going to escape.

From their positions, the Australians could not see the Cathay Building with the Japanese flag flying over it. Bennett had decided not to mention the surrender to anyone but the officers until it was announced by Percival. There were plenty of rumours many of them probably fuelled by reports on the bush telegraph that three British officers had been seen walking through the Japanese lines that morning waving a white flag. But Bennett found the men cheerful and optimistic and contemptuous of the very idea of surrendering.

At the headquarters of 2/20th Battalion, in a beautifully furnished house, Bennett took afternoon tea in fine bone china cups. One of his officers, on being told about the surrender broke down and wept. From the top storey of the house, he later worked out his line of escape which he had already decided would begin that night.

The official announcement was not made until Percival got back from Bukit Timah and had issued his orders to his senior officers. The cease fire would come into effect at 8.30 that night, in about half an hour's time, when every unit would gather into one area and lay down their weapons and equipment. The AIF's artillery was to be delivered to a playing field.

The troops were told that the reason for the surrender was to prevent the wholesale slaughter of the civilian population and because the public utilities and health had almost completely broken down. Their own position as a fighting force was also hopeless.

Most of the Australians could not believe that walking voluntarily into prison was even an option that their officers would have considered. Only days before they had been told that they would remain in their positions and if necessary die there and almost to a man they found this more acceptable than the disgrace of simply giving up.

Someone said this was the first time that Australian soldiers had ever laid down their arms and that made them even more miserable. And then they told themselves that it was a British order to surrender and a British general who had got them into that mess. Somehow that made it a little easier to convince themselves that they were not letting Australia down through any action of their own. There was a lot of guilt to be worked out.

Frank Hole, a bren gunner with the 2/20th, was one of many Australians who had saved one bullet or one grenade for themselves. He had a grenade and he had worked out that he would fight his way back, in a last ditch situation, to an air raid shelter in the garden where he was dug in. Then he would wait for the Japs to come, pull the pin on the grenade at the last moment and take as many with him as he could.

Two Queenslanders with the 2/26th were so outraged when they heard that they were to be taken prisoner that they immediately set off northwards on foot, insisting that they were somehow going to find their way home to fight another day. They were never seen again. And a patrol of Gordon Highlanders, attached to the AIF, were so disgusted that they wanted to go straight back out on patrol and stay there until their last round of ammunition and last grenade had been used.

Perhaps the hardest thing to bear, after the guilt, was the realisation that all their fighting and suffering, all their determination to win and all those casualties and deaths had been for nothing.

Soon after eight o'clock they heard singing and cheering from the Japanese lines as news of the surrender reached them and there was a moment of consternation when the Australians thought the Japanese were psyching themselves up for a final attack. They sent a message back to Bennett asking what they were to do if the Japanese broke through before 8.30 when the surrender formally came into force. Bennett told them that they would still be at war and could therefore take 'severe action' to check any enemy advance.

Privately, he had grave fears that the Japanese would run amok when they knew that the Australians were unarmed and helpless, but it was one fear that turned out to be groundless. The Japanese officers kept a tight rein on their men, at least for that day.

At 8.30 there was an eerie and frightening silence as the guns, for the first time in many weeks, fell silent. At the Australian Field Hospital the surgeons and medical teams has been working for two days with only water and buckets for sterilising. One of the surgeons remembers that they found the sudden silence after weeks of constant and deafening noise almost more unsettling than the artillery fire. They all knew that it meant a surrender.

A great pall of smoke was rising from the bomb-damaged city and flames shot into the sky from the oil tanks, but the Australians spent the night talking, as though they did not trust the Japanese not to run through them and wanted to have their eyes open when they came. In a brief pause in the conversation at 2/20th headquarters, a Japanese startled them by suddenly giving three loud and clear *banzais*. He must have been very close but there was no gun fire and the Japanese observed the truce scrupulously.

All that night they saw no Japanese and they talked endlessly about what was likely to happen to them. Some were so shocked at the idea of captivity that they could hardly speak about it, while a few got drunk on the wine, of which there were still copious amounts.

There was a real fear about how the Japanese would treat them in prison and what their fate would be. They had been listening to stories about Japanese brutality and torture for so long that they were willing to believe every word and more. Most knew somebody who had first-hand knowledge of the atrocities they had committed in Shanghai.

And there were other fears, without substance but no less real for that. Many of them firmly believed that prisoners-of-war were always sterile after their captivity and this bothered many of them almost more than the idea of what the Japanese might do to them.

Technically they had to lay down their arms by 9.30 that night, but it was not until the following morning that this actually occurred. In the meantime many of them threw the bolts of their machine guns down wells or deep into the jungle, while others changed rifle bolts in the vague hope that this would in some way make the weapons less efficient for the Japanese.

Next morning they had a good breakfast and crammed their packs with food. At 8.00 they assembled as a unit and were addressed by their old commanding officer, Brigadier 'Black Jack' Galleghan. A much respected commander whom his men thought was on his way back to Australia, Galleghan became the dominant figure among the Australians when they got to Changi. He harangued them on the need to hold together as a fighting unit in prison as they had on the battlefield and to hold together through the certain dangers that lay ahead of them. And less accurately he told them that he thought they would be prisoners-of-war for only a few months.

By 10.00 they had been disarmed and there was nothing to do but wait for the Japanese to come for them. A few late arrivals came in with reports that they had better hide their watches or the Japs would take them: some, they said, had watches on each wrist and half way up both arms.

All that Monday, however, nobody came near the Australians and many of them had still not seen a live Japanese since they started fighting on the island. It was a most disturbing day for the men. Conditioned to feel naked when they were parted from their weapons for only a few minutes, the knowledge that they had lost them altogether and that the Japanese, always at their cruellest in time of victory, were just out of sight in the trees was very disconcerting. The few Japanese that some of them did see looked positively evil in their drab uniforms, boots and little cloth caps.

Very few had escaped although no specific orders about that had been given. On the Monday they laid down their weapons they were told not to escape because it was too dangerous. Had Percival not suppressed Wavell's order many more might have attempted to leave. If Bennett wasn't as conspicuous as usual, only a handful of officers knew that their Divisional Commander was already well on his way to freedom.

On Tuesday orders arrived that the 15 000 Australians at Tanglin would be marched that day to their prison camp at Changi. By then anything positive was welcome. As they marched through the outskirts of Singapore, sentries stared at them without any apparent interest and one or two presented arms in the traditional compliment to troops who have just surrendered.

Before they left Tanglin, they had been warned that all Japanese soldiers, no matter what their rank, had to be saluted and before many days passed they had learned that the punishment for failing to do this was likely to be a vicious punch in the mouth or a savage backhander across the face.

For fit soldiers the 16-km march to Changi should have taken no more than two and a half hours, but the journey was a nightmare of stopping and starting as tens of thousands of other prisoners took their place in the long and humiliating procession making its way into captivity. It was after dark when the head of the column passed through the camp gates at Changi and after midnight when the last man was in.

They were not hassled on the journey, but the Japanese gave them no food all day. They ate the rations which Gordon Bennett had insisted they carry and drank from water taps or from cups given to them by sympathetic Chinese along the way. They had initially been ordered to carry ten days' rations with them, but Percival had complained that they were too exhausted and in the end the Japanese relented and allowed them to send the rations by truck.

The wounded in the base hospitals were also taken out to Changi by truck and a few of the more enterprising healthy soldiers managed to avoid the long march and conjure up their own transport. The last surviving men of the Argylls had somehow found enough trucks to carry them all into captivity and they made the journey with their piper playing them along every metre of the road.

A British Army captain, gaoled by a civilian court for accepting bribes from Chinese in exchange for supply contracts and then released when fighting began, had lost none of his skills. As healthy as anyone on the march, he still managed to persuade someone that he was too ill to walk and needed a place in a truck. He probably took the place of someone who really needed it for there were many whom the Japanese did not consider to be sick enough to warrant providing transport for, and for them the march to Changi was a terrible ordeal.

There were fears for those who fell by the wayside because of the tales they had heard about Japanese guards and so there were hundreds of helping hands extended and many whose comrades carried them the whole way on their backs along that interminable road. As they passed through the gates at Changi, their quartermaster staff were waiting with a hot meal and that night many of them lay down where they were and fell asleep exhausted.

Morale among the Australians was as low as it had ever been. On top of all their other worries, many were now suffering from bacillary dysentery, the scourge that has followed armies through history and that decimated Napoleon's forces in the Russian campaign. They were hardly inside the prison gates before men were digging the great bore-hole latrines around which a hundred men would defecate before crawling off for a few minutes to give someone else a chance to take their place. In such basic ways did nearly 100 000 men begin their long ordeal in captivity.

A few did not make the march to Changi but chose instead to try and escape. One who did try and who brought a storm of controversy down on himself in the process, which might all have been avoided if Wavell's last order had been passed on, was Gordon Bennett. His decision to escape was not made on the spur of the moment for as long before as the withdrawal over the causeway, he had confided to his chief signals officer that the Allies would now be 'caught like rats in a trap' and added, 'but they won't get me'.

As the end came closer he planned the escape with the same care that he prepared for every military exercise. He had decided to take two people with him, Major Charles Moses, his staff officer, and

Lieutenant Gordon Walker, his ADC and both would have to be left to take care of much of the detail if he was to be ready to leave in the very short time possible — between the surrender and the march into Changi.

As soon as he returned to his quarters after his last inspection of the lines, he began to make his final preparations. He ate an unwanted meal, burned his papers and sorted out his kit; and when confirmation arrived that the surrender would be at 8.30, only half an hour later, he told Moses to be ready to leave within the hour. If the Japanese arrived before he had finished his last duties, he would hide until the coast was clear.

Moses had found a Chinese man who was willing to take them to Sumatra. It was not a route that Bennett had given serious thought to before because he had discounted the possibility of still being able to find a boat on Singapore, but he welcomed it. It would save a 200-km trek through the jungle and the enemy's lines. Until now, he had always planned on going north to Malacca or Port Dickson where he was confident they would find a boat.

It was ten o'clock before he had finished saying his farewells and when he got back to his quarters he found Moses and Walker waiting for him with the car and the Chinese. They drove quickly towards the city, now dark and silent and acrid with the smell of burning rubber. Once they were stopped by some men of the Gordon Highlanders who wanted to know if it was true that the war was over and when Bennett assured them that it was, they vanished into the night.

They had expected the Japanese to be in occupation of the city already, but there wasn't a soul. The streets were deserted and once the Gordons had gone, they made good time, steering precariously past the bomb craters and fallen telegraph poles.

At a point along the coast near Kallang Airfield, their guide told them to stop the car and he led them down towards the water on foot. They had gone only a few steps when they ran straight into an Indian patrol which had not been told that the fighting had stopped. While Bennett stayed by the car, Moses and Walker went in search of the officer of the guard. Then with him giving them safe conduct, they passed through the sentry positions keeping very quiet because Japanese officers had just been reported in the area.

At last they were within sight of the water's edge and Bennett felt a surge of excitement as the reality of what he was doing suddenly struck home. They picked their way along a rough track until they came to a wharf where the guide said the boat should have been — only it wasn't there! The wharf was empty.

The guide now left them, refusing any payment, and Bennett gave him his staff car which must have been a dangerous gift to accept. They could see some sampans about 50 m off-shore and Walker, stripping off his uniform, dived into the phosphorescent sea and swam out to them. He found they were firmly lashed together and he had to cut the lashing on three of them before the boat he wanted finally came free. He brought it inexpertly into the shore.

They threw in their belongings, scrambled down the piers of the jetty and were just pulling away when a group of men ran on to the wharf shouting and waving. Bennett's first thought was that they were Japanese, but he could make out a few words of English and when they took the sampan back into the edge, they found that it was a party of eight planters all wanting to escape.

They took them all on board and with the sampan listing badly set off for a second time, moving in what they thought was the direction that would take them out of the harbour.

The harbour was so full of sampans that it was difficult to find a way through them, but they finally emerged from the jam near a *tongkan* which they boarded. On board they found two men, looking wet and ill, who had swum out from shore and they explained miserably that two others with them had drowned when they couldn't swim the distance.

The owner of the *tongkan* was a Chinese who was busily occupied with his opium pipe when they first saw him. In fact he was busily occupied with his pipe every time they saw him which nearly brought about their downfall. He refused to take them to Sumatra saying that he could only get opium in Singapore.

Including the crew, there were nineteen people on board and an inspection of the boat revealed an arsenal of anti-aircraft ammunition. They haggled with him and eventually persuaded him to take them to Sumatra for $150 down and more when they arrived safely. Finally at 1.00 a.m. they set sail.

Fortune stayed with them as they sailed gingerly through the minefield, designed for ships of much deeper draught. They were just congratulating themselves that they must be clear of it when the owner without warning turned his boat around and began heading back through the minefield to Singapore. This time they didn't argue and they threw him into his quarters and left a Malayan in command who had been picked up as navigator.

The only map they had was a page ripped out of a school atlas with a scale of about 160 km to the centimetre; and the water supply was so low that they had to ration themselves to a tumbler in the morning and another in the evening.

By the evening of the 18th, they had successfully crossed the Malacca Strait without sighting the Japanese. The following day a fast launch came alongside which took them aboard. They finally stepped ashore on 21 February at Jambi, a provincial capital in north-east Sumatra some 300 km upstream on the Batanghari River. With only four litres of fuel left in the tank, their hazardous journey was over without serious mishap.

The following day the Dutch officials at Jambi arranged for Bennett, Moses and Walker to be taken across the island to Padang on the west coast where Bennett would arrange for a Catalina to take them to Batavia. From there it was a safe run down to Broome in Western Australia.

Wavell rang while they were in Pandang to ask if the reports coming out of Singapore about the number of Australian troops deserting were accurate and he was not reassured by Bennett's answer.

The three men finally arrived back on Australian soil at 5.00 p.m. on 27 February, ten days after Bennett's division had marched off to Changi. If he now expected a warm welcome when he got back to Melbourne's Victoria Barracks, he was sadly disappointed. Expecting to be received with warmth and congratulations after his escape, he went straight to call on General Sturdee, the Chief of the General Staff.

After a few minutes desultory conversation that was decidedly chilly, Sturdee told him bluntly that his escape was ill-advised and that he should have stayed with his men. Sturdee then turned away from him rudely and went on with his work, leaving Bennett standing in the middle of the room to make his own way out. No other member of the Military Board came out to see him.

Their attitude made no sense to him. Even if his main reason for escaping *was* to avoid going into captivity, no less important was that he could give the General Staff a vital first-hand account of the fight for Malaya and Singapore that would be invaluable in planning future operations. Only a month before, this same Military Board that was now spurning him had instructed all ranks that if they were captured, their first duty was to escape; and that escape was always easier in the early stages of captivity.

But the Board members were the only people who were hostile and when Bennett attended a meeting of the War Cabinet, Prime Minister John Curtin was friendly and gave a short speech assuring him that the government had complete confidence in him and that he personally would have done the same thing. Then without consulting Sturdee, Curtin issued a press statement in which he said '...We have expressed to Major-General Bennett our confidence in him. His leadership and conduct were in complete conformity with his duty to the men under his command and to his country. He remained with his men until the end, completed all formalities in connection with the surrender, and then took the opportunity and risk of escaping.' It was a glowing vindication of what he had done.

For nearly four years no formal action was taken over the affair although the debate continued. Bennett was made Commander of III Corps and transferred to Perth, but he was never given another posting. With the passing of time, the facts became garbled so that Bennett became the villain for things he had never done. It was even said that Bennett, who was about the most fearless commander in the AIF, had abandoned his troops.

There was a very large body of opinion, however, which thought that Bennett had been very shabbily treated and that the Army had behaved disgracefully towards a brave soldier who had shown more imagination than all the other senior officers combined. He had been an inspiration to his troops in a battle zone where inspiration was sadly wanting.

On the other side, Bennett's critics pointed out that the Australians badly needed someone to look after their rights, to negotiate decent conditions and just to be seen to be there, suffering alongside them. They said it didn't need Bennett to tell the generals about a campaign that was now fought and lost; but that it was very embarrassing to other Australian officers that Percival, who presumably had the same opportunities to escape as Bennett, chose to stay with his men.

Canvassing the feeling today among Bennett's men, not one former private or NCO was critical of Bennett's flight, while not a single officer thought he did the right thing.

With his career now obviously in limbo, Bennett retired in 1944 but the dispute refused to die down. In 1945 it was still simmering in Australia and overseas. There were repeated demands for an official investigation, most loudly from Bennett himself. General Blamey, whose antipathy towards Bennett was widely known, wanted to hold a private enquiry but the government, wanting no more secrecy on the affair, decided to appoint a Royal Commission. The Commissioner was a South Australian Supreme Court Judge, Mr Justice Ligertwood.

The Royal Commission's finding was almost as unsatisfactory as the situation that existed before Ligertwood began hearing the evidence. He found that Bennett's bravery 'unremitting devotion to duty and acceptance of personal risks in the most advanced operational areas', were beyond dispute and that Bennett had not been actuated to escape by a desire to secure his own safety, 'but had acted from a sense of high patriotism and according to what he conceived to be his duty to his country.'

Indeed Ligertwood went on, 'He genuinely believed that Australia was in peril and that it was of vital importance to the safety of the country that he should return to take a leading part in its defence (and) he did bring back valuable information to Australia which was used in training of the AIF in jungle warfare...I am fully convinced of General Bennett's good faith.'

After a preamble like that one might imagine that the Royal Commissioner could have closed the book, but far from it. Having said that all Bennett's motives were good and that the information he brought back was valuable, Ligertwood proceeded to find *against* him. With a piece of legal legerdemain so contrived that lawyers still look on it in wonderment forty years later, he found that even though the surrender document had been signed by Percival to come into effect at 8.30, and even though the Allied forces and the Japanese had ceased fire and the Allies had laid down their arms by the time he left at 10.00, nevertheless he had committed an infraction of international law. He was not at that particular moment legally a prisoner-of-war until he was behind bars: and the moment *that* happened he would have had a positive obligation to try to escape. Until then he had an obligation to stay in command of his men and he failed to do so.

If Ligertwood was right surrender did not occur when the Allies laid down their weapons and waited for the Japanese to take them into captivity. And if that is the case it raises the very important question of what exactly their status was if they were neither combatants nor prisoners-or-war. It is important because prisoners-of-war are protected by certain conventions and if Ligertwood's very narrow interpretation was correct, the Japanese could have treated the Australians in almost any way they chose and with whatever barbarity they chose to do it.

As one commentator, a former Deputy Judge Advocate General, observed, 'A soldier is taught to fight and if captured or surrendered...to escape in order to be able to fight again another day. If that honourable code is to lose its simplicity in a maze of legal subtlety, Australia's soldiers will remember the alleged miscalculations made by General Bennett and they will hesitate in the early stages of capture or surrender, which in the past soldiers have always been advised is the best time to escape.'

Even more unfortunate is that many people remember this tough, abrasive and difficult general, who would have died a dozen times for his men if he was called on, and who showed rare imagination and courage, as a man who walked out on the men he loved and abandoned them to their fate in Changi. That is a very unfair assessment when, except on one small technicality of international law, he was totally exonerated.

Gordon Bennett died in August 1962 when he was seventy-five, still swearing that if he had to go through it all again, he would still escape.

The double-standard which had made it acceptable and respectable for many other senior officers to attempt to escape on the last boats leaving the island, in almost identical circumstances to those for which Gordon Bennett was later branded at fault (they were chosen for the information they could give and the contribution they could make to the on-going war effort), had many tragic endings.

Vice-Admiral E. J. Spooner, Commanding the Naval Staff at Singapore, and Air Vice-Marshal Pulford, who had been the senior air officer for so long, left on a patrol boat but were forced ashore on a deserted malarial island in the Tuju Group, 50 km north of Banka Island where the Japanese performed many atrocities on fleeing Europeans. With few stores and no doctor, eighteen of them died, including Spooner and Pulford, before the survivors were found and taken prisoner by the Japanese.

As Pulford had said his farewell to Percival, he had remarked, prophetically for Percival, 'I suppose you and I will be blamed for this, but God knows we have done our best with what we have been given.'

With all their prisoners-of-war safely behind bars, the Japanese could round up the civilians who had to be taken out of circulation. The main body of Japanese troops was kept out of the city for a week, partly to protect the citizens and partly because there was still a risk of disease until the streets and bomb damage had been cleared up.

The *Straits Times* appeared for the last time on Saturday 14 February, printed on a single sheet of paper. It included an official warning to the population to disperse by day into the open spaces nearest to them, preferably 'where you can be hidden from air observation'. It was a necessary warning for the Japanese pilots, who were constantly patrolling over the city, fired at almost everything that moved.

There was a last rather weary attempt to bolster the now almost moribund morale of the beleagured city. 'Our troops are disputing every attempt to advance further towards the heart of Singapore,' the *Times* said. 'It is understood that our artillery engaged some of the enemy forces with considerable success, inflicting about a hundred casualties.' There was still no mention or warning of the fact that the water supply had almost run out and that an epidemic was inevitable if the greatest care was not taken in using what water remained.

A cable arrived that same day from the Secretary of State for the Colonies in London, addressed to 'All those who are so gallantly and doggedly helping in the defence of Singapore.' The Minister sent the people of Singapore his grateful thanks for 'their devoted assistance' and added that he knew they would continue to do everything they could to defend the city. They would have preferred the aircraft and reinforcements they had been promised for so long by London.

Only one more English-language newspaper would appear before the Japanese took it over as a propaganda sheet for their own purposes. On Sunday 15 February, the last day of Singapore's struggle for survival, the *Sunday Times* appeared under a stark banner with a 2.5 cm-high injunction from the Governor: 'Singapore must stand: it *shall* stand.' The story said that the Allies were 'disputing every attempt by the Japs to advance further towards the heart of Singapore town.'

As they collected their dead and tried to eke out some kind of an existence in the ruins of their city, the people no longer even cared, let alone believed, it to be true.

Singapore was a disaster area. Buildings had collapsed on top of their occupants and there were no labour gangs to try and free them; and the bombing continued mercilessly leaving the roads pock-marked with unrepaired craters. Anti-aircraft gun-fire had virtually ceased to exist.

The civil hospital had now been without water for twenty-four hours and if the precise daily casualty tally was unknown, what was certain was that it was far beyond the resources of anyone to cope with.

Many reported afterwards that there was a strange feeling of time being in suspended animation on their last night of freedom. They suddenly felt neither fear nor even apprehension, only relief that the carnage and the bombing were finally over and that from now on their lives, if not their freedom, were assured.

Some sat down to a Surrender Dinner — steak and kidney pie, Christmas pudding and strawberries and cream were one man's choice. But they ate it not as the final breakfast of a condemned man, so much as with the excitement of schoolboys enjoying a guilty feast at the end of term — not sure what the holidays would bring, but certain that it had to be better than the term just past.

Everyone was putting together the things they wanted to take into internment. Some had large packs and several suitcases, believing that they would be driven to captivity. Changi, with the gaol and complex of barracks, seemed the most likely place where they would be held. As it was 15 km from town, they assumed that they would have to be driven there.

At Robinsons department store, management had obeyed the instruction that every receptacle must be filled with water and this had included the baths on the showroom floor. On the last day, a dozen men lay back in these tubs, scrubbing themselves with soap which they had found in the ladies' hair-dressing salon, and prepared to go into captivity clean.

Sir Shenton Thomas broadcast to the population for the last time on Monday. With Japanese soldiers standing beside him to ensure that he said only what had been written in his approved speech, he told the people to remain calm and to stay off the streets. All European civilians were to make their way to Raffles Hotel where they would be held pending further Japanese instructions. For the rest of the day the Europeans continued to drift into the hotel where their names were recorded. There were still few Japanese in evidence and the organisation was being handled by members of the administration.

On that Sunday night, while the defeated and dispirited troops and civilians waited inside the perimeter wondering what their fate would be, Yamashita's 25th Army remained outside. His concern was partly to prevent looting and bloody revenge on the Chinese civilians in particular, but principally to reduce the risk of his men being infected if an epidemic broke out.

Everything looked and smelled filthy and from under the rubble of bombed buildings came the smell of putrefying bodies that had not been recovered. What little water still remained was polluted by sewage from broken mains and open drains.

The only Japanese permitted into the city on the first night were the Kempei Tai, the military police, and auxiliary Kempeis drawn from the Japanese 5th Division who turned out to be even more brutal than the Kempei themselves. In addition there were the thousand Allied troops who had been allowed to remain under arms to patrol the city and maintain law and order. In fact they encountered few problems. Shock at the knowledge that the Japanese now controlled the city and sheer fear at the sight of Japanese soldiers in the streets produced a very calm atmosphere.

The following morning, substantial numbers of Japanese entered the city for the first time and Yamashita, to remind the people that he had conquered by force and would suppress them again by force if necessary, put on a formidable display of power and sent 175 tanks rumbling through the streets while his aircraft patrolled constantly overhead.

At about 8.00 on Monday morning, a car flying the Rising Sun pulled up in front of the prison gates and a man got out and called in Japanese, 'Any Japanese inside? The British have surrendered.'

From the other side of the gates, Mamoru Shinozaki shouted back with delight that there were and within an hour the Kempei Tai were in the gaol and the thirty Japanese being held there were on their way out.

The defeat of Singapore had been completed so quickly — thirty days sooner than the planners had forecast — that the civil administration which was to move in to run the city was not ready. Caretakers therefore looked after it while arrangements were being made to speed up the arrival of the new administration. British and Australian firemen, nurses, doctors, water engineers, health and sanitary workers were all ordered to stay at their posts until their Japanese counterparts arrived. It was only the efforts of the civilian engineers, who had stayed at their posts until well after the surrender, which ensured that even minimal utility services were maintained.

The Japanese acted immediately to make their presence felt. The clock tower on the town hall, for example, was changed to Tokyo time and remained like that until the Japanese surrender. The Japanese always used Tokyo time in their overseas theatres of war.

The island and city were renamed Syonan, which meant Brilliant South, and various headquarters were established in buildings around the city. Yamashita established his own headquarters at Raffles College, today the University of Singapore, while Percival's bunker at Fort Canning was taken over as Defence Headquarters by Major General Kawamura, the Commandant of Singapore. The Orchard Road YMCA became notorious as the headquarters of the Kempei Tai and its torturers under Colonel Oishi. Yamashita, Kawamura and Oishi would all walk up the thirteen steps to the gallows at Changi after the surrender.

The Japanese immediately began using their own currency. It quickly became known as 'banana money' after the bunch of bananas in the picture on the ten dollar note, designed to encourage the local people to grow more food. The new currency had exactly the same value as the old. Both were equally good tender in the shops throughout the occupation. But there was a rush to get rid of the old currency that had not been burned because people thought that it would be worthless. (In the same way they hurried to get rid of the Japanese money towards the end of the occupation.)

The Japanese began looting immediately and found that they were competing with the Chinese who had been doing it since before the surrender had even been signed. The Chinese arrived in the more expensive European residential areas, running the gauntlet of the blitz and the defending soldiers, in vehicles and on foot, carrying long poles to carry their loot away.

The Japanese swiftly put an end to this competition by beheading eight Chinese looters caught red-handed and displaying their heads on spikes in small wooden trays at eight major road intersections.

Immediately after the capitulation, there were many surprises for the Europeans waiting to go into captivity, as local people suddenly appeared wearing the uniform and sword of a Japanese officer. Most were Japanese who had left before the Japanese landings or had gone into hiding, but others had been there all the time, some pretending to be Thais or Malays, others lying undercover in the city. Generally, these officers did not abuse their old friendships.

The line between collaboration with an enemy and co-operation is often uncomfortably thin and never more so than in Singapore, where the residents of the island, whatever their race, were totally vulnerable and under no illusions at all about what the Japanese would do to them if they were even slow to respond to a command.

Although she herself was briefly and wrongly accused of collaboration by other Europeans, Cynthia Koek, the quintessential patriot, never swerved from her belief that 'Many people who collaborated had absolutely no choice and those silly people who didn't — and I admired them greatly if they refused — lost everything.'

One European Jew who did collaborate to save his life and who worked in the Police Department for the Japanese, said that it was his experience that 'The Chinese wouldn't betray you no matter what the Japs were doing to them, but you couldn't trust any of the Malayans or the Eurasians.'

On the grand scale, thousands of Indian soldiers defected and joined what became known as the Indian National Army, turning their guns against the British and fighting alongside the Japanese.

The Malayans on the whole received a warm welcome, but the Chinese were terrorised. Almost immediately after the surrender and the Japanese occupation of the city, the order went out for thousands of Chinese men to be rounded up so that they could be purged of any 'anti-Nippon elements'. This included anyone suspected of having supported the mainland Chinese by word or deed during the Sino-Japanese struggle.

Operation Clean-up, as it was known, was supervised by the Kempei Tai and auxiliary Kempeis. All Chinese men between the ages of eighteen and fifty were ordered to concentrate at five assembly points where they were interrogated. They were kept at these places with little or no shelter against the sweltering sun, no toilets and no water in their tens of thousands while they were checked and classified in a mockery of an investigation.

The Kempei's criteria for deciding whether a Chinese warranted punishment were arbitrary and cruel. Those who wrote their names in English and not Chinese (many were illiterate in Chinese) could apologise to the Kempei or were purged. To write in English was construed as meaning that they must be pro-British and therefore dangerous.

Anyone with tattoo marks was arbitrarily classified as a member of a secret society, while those who were reasonably well-dressed were assumed to be working for the British and therefore to be suspect. Not to bow deeply enough could mean punishment, while to bow too deeply could mean servility and so an attempt to cover up a hidden secret.

Those who were put aside for punishment were all massacred. By the Kempei Tai's own figures, they killed six thousand in this one purge, and the Chinese have put the figure as much higher. The killings took place at the seaside at Ponggol, on the north-east coast of the island; at the beach near the tenth mile-post on the Changi Road; and in the sea off Pulau Belakang Mati, today the much publicised recreation island of Sentosa, off the coast from Singapore City.

Most of the victims were thrown into the sea from boats and machine-gunned to death, or were made to wade into the water until they were waist deep and were again machine-gunned. Off Sentosa, the Japanese recorded, the sea turned red.

Many of the soldiers responsible for these atrocities were peasants from the west of Japan. Superstitious Japanese still maintain that the atomic bomb attacks on Hiroshima and Nagasaki were the vengeance of God for the slaughter of these Chinese. By strange coincidence, the 5th Division which supplied the Kempei Tai was raised in Hiroshima and the 18th Division which carried out many of the executions came from Nagasaki.

Imprisonment itself began for most of the Europeans on the following day, Tuesday the 17th. By 10.00 a.m. two thousand men and three hundred women and their children had been lined up in the blazing sun on the Cricket Club *padang*, the wide recreation ground in the centre of the city. The men were at one end and the women and children at the other and they were allowed no contact with each other.

The women in particular were hopelessly unprepared for the ordeal of standing in the glare of the sun with no protection. They had arrived in light clothes and shoes — some even with high heels — and many of them had no hats to protect them and were leading or carrying young children or babies. There wasn't even a breeze over the *padang* to temper the heat.

The men stood with their pathetic bundles of possessions and some of the women had brought prams to push their belongings in and all had been told that they would be severely restricted in the amount of luggage they could take with them.

In a group apart from the others were high-ranking government officials led by Sir Shenton Thomas in newly pressed clean white ducks. He was adamant that in spite of his age and the likelihood, he believed, that the Japanese would give him preferential treatment out of respect for his position, he would take everything handed out to the others. For all his failings during the conduct of the war and for all his lack of colour and charisma when both were so needed, nobody ever questioned that Thomas was a man of great personal courage and integrity.

His concern that he would be singled out for special treatment was correct, though not in the way that he had anticipated. The Japanese decreed that he was 'a special case to be humiliated' and though many senior officials were driven to the first camp, he was specifically ordered to walk the whole distance.

Those who expected to find transport waiting for them were disappointed and were told that they would have to walk to Katong, about 5 km away. Katong was then by the water (reclaimed land has put it some distance from the sea today), beyond Kallang airfield. Almost nobody had come prepared for such a walk. By the time they arrived there, they were exhausted, their feet blistered, their shoes worn through and their noses and faces burned raw.

At Katong the men were put into the police compound while the women went into Chinese houses and there they were given their first taste of the food that would become part of their lives for the next three years, a dirty bowl of rice. Lady Thomas, too ill to leave her bed, was taken to a Japanese military hospital. Somehow, with considerable help from the spy Mamoru Shinozaki, she survived her captivity.

Not all the civilians heard Thomas's broadcast calling on them to go to Raffles and not all of those who heard it had any intention of obeying. Edward and Cynthia Koek had stayed at their refuge at Raffles Place until the last moment with several of their friends. It suddenly occurred to them that the last place a group of Europeans ought to be taking refuge in was the former offices of the Japanese NYK Company which they had taken over for their little hospital.

They drove back to Tanglin in the Koek's seven-seater Hudson and were so anxious to get out that they left many of their possessions in the office safe, including some valuable jewellery which they never saw again.

They drove along River Valley Road and passed a long column of Japanese vehicles and troops heading in the other direction. The men were marching in strict formation and the most eerie part was that nobody took the slightest notice of them. They passed Japanese military policemen directing the traffic, but received not so much as a glance. 'We might have been invisible,' Cynthia Koek recalled afterwards.

Their house at Tanglin was a big old bungalow, standing on a site which today has eight houses on it near the present Marco Polo Hotel. They stayed there for three days not daring to go outside. Several times Japanese officers came to the house but the Koeks and six other Europeans with them were treated courteously. The Japanese drank tea with them, listened to their records and left. It was unnerving.

Some of these officers who came warned them that the invasion forces would shortly be leaving Singapore and that in their place would come other less tolerant soldiers. 'Just be warned,' one of them said. 'As we go out to other campaigns, the troops who come in will come increasingly from the lower classes until you get down to the peasants. And when the very lowest class of peasant comes in, be careful. They are filled up with propaganda, they will hate you because you are white and they will do everything they can to insult you and they will beat you. When that happens, you will be glad that you are in detention.'

Sure enough, that same afternoon, new men who were very different came to the house. They were in the sitting room when the door burst open and half a dozen Japanese rushed in pointing their rifles at them and shouting.

'You bad people,' one of them kept saying. 'You bad people. Why didn't you give yourselves up?'

'Why should we? We live here.' Cynthia Koek retorted defiantly. 'This is our place.'

The Japanese shook his head. 'Aren't you frightened of us?'

'No, not a bit,' she told him firmly, though in truth she was scared out of her wits. 'I'm not frightened of you. None of us is frightened of you. Why should we be?'

The Japanese shook his head even more vigorously. 'Ah, yes, but we will kill you. Our sword, see. This side dreadfully sharp. Poong, ping! Head come off.' And he went through a fearsome charade to make his point.

Inwardly freezing, Cynthia Koek said coolly, 'Good. Head come off very quickly. No hurt. Come off slowly, very bad.'

The Japanese stared at her and then he pointed to her one leg as though he suddenly understood everything. 'Ah, you got one leg. You very brave woman.'

She shook her head. 'I'm not brave at all, but I'm not frightened.'

'You none of you frightened?' he asked, looking round at the others who were ashen-faced.

'No,' they lied quickly. 'Of course not. Why should we be frightened?'

The Japanese suddenly sat down on the sofa. 'You got tea?' he demanded loudly. In their relief the women moved so fast to get to the kitchen that they collided in the door. An hour later, after sipping tea from bone china cups and listening to Beethoven's Fifth on the Koek's gramophone, they trooped out into the garden.

This alarming introduction to the Japanese at least served one purpose. They had learned the important psychological lesson that it was not only possible to stand up to the Japanese but that they respected you if you did. It would serve them well in the coming months and years.

But early next morning they had yet another visit which reminded them that they could never be sure about anything when dealing with the Japanese. Soon after six, a second party arrived and this time they crashed into the bedroom with fixed bayonets, shouting out loudly. The conversation opened in the same way as the one the day before.

'You all very bad people. You all get up.'

Cynthia Koek found her voice first. 'Very well,' she agreed calmly, 'you go outside and we dress.'

But they refused to move and the Koeks had to dress in front of them. The same routine was happening in the other bedrooms.

The Japanese ordered them to get into the Hudson and to follow them and they took them to a big house in Orange Grove Road Estate where the Shangri La Hotel stands today. Unfortunately for Koek, the moment the car arrived at the front door, the engine stalled and nothing he could do would persuade it to start again. The Japanese, convinced that he had deliberately sabotaged it, were furious and ordered him to stay with the car until it started. If it didn't start, they promised him in tones that strongly suggested they meant it, they would kill him. Koek, who had a chauffeur and knew nothing about car engines, asked if he could fetch his driver but they refused: they kept him outside for the rest of the day, in between interrogations, Though the car never started, he kept his life.

They kept them all at the interrogation centre from 8.00 a.m. until late evening with nothing to eat or drink all day. The interrogation was repetitive and dealt mainly with trivial personal questions. Although they were not physically mistreated, they learned a few more painful lessons.

They did not know, for example, that they had to bow to officers and when the first one came along, they stayed sitting on their chairs and looked at him. A soldier then went down the line hitting them all in the face as though it was a slapstick. They had no idea why he was hitting them until the soldier went through a pantomime of jumping up and bowing when an officer walked past.

They got the message and when the next officer arrived, they stood up in a line and bowed respectfully. Unfortunately they stayed standing and they all got another slap in the face for not sitting down again. By the time the day was over, their faces were very sore and their ears were ringing from being shouted at incessantly.

All the civilians, European and Asian, were in constant trouble trying to remember all the things that annoyed the Japanese and for which the almost invariable penalty was a hard slap across the face. If they whispered, for example, they would be immediately hit because it was assumed they had a secret to hide. If they closed a door tight it was likely to be construed as a personal insult.

At last the Koeks and their companions were told that they must go and have themselves interned. The only difficulty was that neither they nor the Japanese knew where the internment camp was. They all piled into a second car that they had come down in and set off to look. They decided not to go anywhere near the city or the long convoy they had seen earlier, and instead they drove to the Singapore Swimming Club which they thought would be an agreeable place to be interned.

When they got there, however, they found a Japanese guard on the door and a young Air Force officer who told them that it was now the officers' mess for Army Air Force Headquarters. He also told them to go away, but then as though remembering how late it was, he looked at his watch, clicked his tongue irritably and called another officer.

'We can't let you go either,' he told them. 'If you are out on the streets after dark, the soldiers will probably attack you and kill you.'

They were on the point of telling him how hungry they were and that they had had nothing to eat since the night before, when an officer came up behind them and in a flawless mid-west American accent apologised and invited them to have dinner with him. In the meantime he found some Nestles milk which he told them to drink to build up their strength.

At dinner, Cynthia Koek discovered that she knew several of his relatives in London and they chatted away over their meal. 'He was absolutely charming,' she recalled. He had been educated at Harvard and he was engaged to an American girl when he was recalled to Japan. He was devastated to think that he might never see her again.

One of the women in their party was a concert pianist and after dinner, she asked the Japanese if they would like her to play to them for her supper. So on the last night of what freedom they had left, they dined with the Japanese in their mess, reminisced about other days far away and then for two hours listened to the piano being exquisitely played for them while they stared into their drinks and wondered whatever would happen to them.

They spent the night in the Swimming Club, but the following day, as courteously as ever, the American-speaking officer told them, 'Now you must go to be interned and from the time we leave this club, we are enemies.'

They said politely that of course they understood and thanked him and then he led them in his own staff car, with a flag fluttering from the bonnet, back through the now crowded streets to the place in Orange Grove Road where they had been questioned the day before.

They were told that they must join the other Europeans in Katong and the Air Force officer drove ahead again while they all followed in the one car. Outside Katong compound, he bid them a courteous good-bye and without another word drove off as though they had never met.

The other civilian men and women were still separated and they too said their farewells to each other. For most of them it would be three years before they saw each other again, apart from a fleeting glimpse.

Other Europeans who were in remoter parts of the island were being rounded up at the same time. The matron of the mental hospital at Choa Chu Kang, 10 km out of town, heard Thomas's broadcast but felt that it was her duty to stay with her patients until the bitter end.

She was left alone for only one day before the Japanese arrived and pushed her roughly outside, ignoring her protests that the patients needed her. They made her walk the whole way into Singapore and as well as giving her no protection against the sun and no water or food, they taunted her constantly, threatening that they were going to pack-rape her and then kill her horribly.

She arrived eventually at Katong and the other European women opened the door of their house, in answer to her soft knock, to find her, in the words of one of them, 'looking like a little drowned cat'. The Japanese had not touched her, but the war was long over before she fully recovered from the ordeal of their intimidation.

The Jews in Singapore were particularly concerned about their fate. They did not know whether the Japanese would treat them in the same way the Germans were doing in Europe and many of them stayed in hiding. The Jewish women in particular were terrified of what would happen to them and some tried to maintain a normal life, pretending to be Eurasian. For a girl that was no protection at all against the Japanese who forced many Eurasian girls into their brothels.

In fact, they never persecuted the Jews because of their race and they treated them strictly according to their nationality. The British Jews were detained, the Iraqi Jews, because Iraq was thought to be sympathetic to Germany at the time, were allowed to stay free. And a number of Jews improved their chances of staying free by collaborating.

On the morning after the Koeks arrived at Katong, the men were forced to march the whole way to Changi, a distance of more than 16 km, in the full heat of the day. Some were old, many were not fit and their wives feared for their safety.

Suddenly the women who were left behind felt very alone and afraid. They had to wait another two days before they learned what was to happen to them and the Japanese told them that they too would have to walk to Changi. They were still wearing the shoes that had so injured their feet on the much shorter march to Katong and few of them had ever walked 16 km in their lives under any conditions.

What few possessions they had been allowed to bring were tied in bags and they limped along under the torturing sun, carrying their most treasured possessions which usually included their photographs. The Japanese had refused to allow them to travel in the cool of the night, fearing that they would try to escape in the darkness.

By the time they reached Changi, their feet were swollen and bleeding and most of them could hardly stand up. A sympathetic Japanese doctor picked many of those up in his car who fell beside the road and drove them to Changi before returning for others who couldn't walk any further.

The men already at Changi had been told that the women were being made to take the same walk as themselves, and they were fearful that some of them would die in the sun. But the women knew that their husbands had done it and they were not going to be beaten. They said to each other, 'When we get to Changi, no matter if we are dying, we'll sing at the top of our voices and we'll let these bastards know what we think of them. We'll let them know that they can't get us down!'

As they came in sight of Changi, they glimpsed the men in the distance, lined up at the wire, and they started singing 'There'll always be an England' at the top of their voices. And they sang and they sang and they were still singing as they limped into their own compound and the men cheered until they were hoarse. And so their captivity began.

Bibliography

Allen, Louis, *Singapore 1941-1942*, Davis-Poynter, London, 1977

Barber, Noel, *Sinister Twilight*, Collins, London, 1968

Caffrey, Kate, *Out in the Midday Sun*, Deutsche, London, 1974

Connell, John, *Wavell, Scholar and Soldier*, Collins, London, 1964

Connell, John & Roberts, Michael, *Wavell, Supreme Commander*, Collins, London, 1969

Legg, F., *The Gordon Bennett Story*, Angus & Robertson, Sydney, 1965

Morrison, Ian, *Malayan Postscript*, Angus & Robertson, Sydney, 1943

Newton, R., *The Grim Glory of the 2/19 Battalion, AIF,* 2/19 Battalion AIF Association, Sydney, 1976

Smyth, Sir John, *Percival and the Tragedy of Singapore*, MacDonald, London, 1971

Tsuji, Masamobu, *Singapore, The Japanese Version* (tr. M. E. Lake), Ure Smith, Sydney, 1960

Wigmore, Lionel, *The Japanese Thrust: Australia in the War of 1939-1945*, Australian War Memorial, Canberra, 1957